Sketchcop

Drawing A Line Against Crime

Michael W. Streed

WILDBLUE
PRESS

WildBluePress.com

SketchCop published by:
WILDBLUE PRESS
1153 Bergen Pkwy Ste I #114
Evergreen, Colorado 80439

WILDBLUE PRESS is registered at the U.S. Patent and Trademark Offices.

978-1-942266-31-0   Trade Paperback
978-1-942266-32-7   eBook ISBN

Book Cover Design and Interior Formatting by Elijah Toten
www.totencreative.com

Editor Mary Kay Wayman

*To my loving, dedicated family and
those I serve in the name of justice.*

Contents

Author's Note

The information in this book is based on actual criminal investigations in which I have taken part. The information has been drawn from my personal memory, recollections and observations. It has been verified wherever possible against additional sources including police reports, news sources and discussions with other people involved in these investigations. Although personal recollections, especially years after the incidents, are rarely an exact reproduction of the facts and conversations, I have done whatever practical to verify each piece of information, including checking with a number of people named in this book. In some cases, the names and other identifying information were changed to protect the anonymity of victims and witnesses. I have divulged no classified or protected materials in presenting my stories. Each case is as I remember it. The facts as I present them are true to the best of my recollection and written with the hope that they will inspire those who follow me to serve in the field of law enforcement.

MICHAEL W. STREED

Acknowledgments

This book is a collection of true crime stories spanning my 35 years of law enforcement experience. Throughout my career, I have been supported by an extraordinarily loving and supportive family. Without them, writing this book would not have been possible. A special thanks to my late wife, Mary Streed, who was the first to suggest I write my stories. After her, my wife Elizabeth "Libby" Streed encouraged me to pick up, resume and refine the book to update stories from my extraordinary career. She has become my greatest inspiration. My parents, Orange Police Chief (Ret.) Wayne and JoAnne Streed, instilled in me a strong commitment to public service and taught me how to treat others.

I am also grateful to be associated with the fine men and women of several world-class law enforcement agencies, including the Los Angeles Police Department, the Long Beach Police Department, the Riverside Police Department, the Orange County Sheriff's Department, the Baltimore Police Department and many, many more. These dedicated public servants have shown their faith in me many times during some of their most difficult investigations, and I greatly appreciate their confidence in my skills.

Others I would like to acknowledge include: Orange Police Chief Robert Gustafson and Cypress Police Chief (Ret.) Jackie Gomez-Whitely, two people who have always taken the time for me and have supported me through several personal and professional trials; Placentia Police Lt. (Ret.) John Chandler, an attorney and dear friend who provided legal advice during the process; Baltimore Police Commissioner Kevin Davis, who recognized my skills and introduced my successes to a greater audience; Baltimore Police Crime Laboratory Director Steven O'Dell, who encouraged me to elevate my work and has been a consistent source of support; Baltimore Police Detective Sgt. Kevin Brown and Detective Thomas Wolf, two great guys, who introduced me to the great city of Baltimore and watched over me while I was there; Steven Jackson, Michael Cordova, Carla Torrisi Jackson, Mackenzie Jackson and the staff of WildBlue Press for having the faith in my writing and storytelling skills and shepherding me through the publishing process; Mary Kay Wayman, my editor, who helped refine my story and make it better; and countless others who are not named but are no less important to my success.

Mostly, I would like to recognize and thank the victims, people whose lives have been forever changed by the ravages of violent crime. For the courage you've shown by coming forward and the trust you've placed by letting me in, we, as a society, will forever be in your debt.

Michael W. Streed – The SketchCop

SketchCop

Drawing A Line Against Crime

MICHAEL W. STREED

Introduction

You don't know me. You probably wouldn't even recognize me if you passed me on the street. However, it's likely that you've seen one of my faces. Maybe you recognize the brand that I've left on the neck of countless criminals I've sketched over the last thirty-five years. Or maybe, until you began reading this book, you never really gave police sketches much thought at all.

Much of my work is spent toiling anonymously behind the scenes of some of the country's most horrifying criminal cases, though sometimes I am called out from behind my sketchpad to deliver a sound bite for a reporter curious about my work.

I find it interesting to be where I am today because my career as a police sketch artist was not planned. It became a secondary duty that paralleled my primary duties as a police officer and investigator.

Once I made the decision to follow my father into the family business, law enforcement, expectations ran high that I would rise into the executive branch of police management, as he did. For over thirty years, my father cast a long shadow across law enforcement in Orange County, California, a patchwork of crowded suburbs, thirty-five miles south of downtown Los Angeles, and there was much pressure for me to succeed. But I had no interest in the day-to-day operation of a police department. I was more interested in pursuing my childhood interest in art. Growing up not far from Anaheim, the home of Disneyland, I dreamed for years about becoming a Disney artist. However, once I was bitten by the "police bug," I was determined to find a way to merge my interest in drawing with my burgeoning law enforcement career.

My successful career as a police sketch artist has long piqued public interest. Some of my sketches have made international headlines, while others, no less important, languish in anonymity.

A mystique surrounds police composite sketches, which involve the merger of art and science. To be successful requires me to assume several roles -- pop psychologist, armchair counselor, artist, scientist and investigator. My job is to mine the memories of crime victims and eyewitnesses and create monsters from them. How I do that is the question I have been asked over and over again.

The secret lies in my ability to merge the details of a victim's memory with the lines and shadows that I lay down on paper. And while it might seem odd that something so powerful could come from nothing more than a few recollections and well-placed scribbles, it's a formula that's helped bring many criminals to justice.

And justice, my friends, is what it's all about.

My career as a police officer was a deliberate choice. Ever since I can remember, I stood up for the weak or those who couldn't protect themselves. While waiting to attend the police academy, I was assigned to the crime prevention unit working with the community on safety and security issues. That is where I first learned to communicate with a wide variety of people from different walks of life.

Later, after becoming a police officer, I sought ways to merge my interest in art with police work. Although I enjoyed playing an adult version of "cops and robbers," I wanted to find a way to distinguish myself in my profession and learn new ways to lock up more bad guys.

One evening, I was home alone eating a frozen dinner while watching a local newscast on television. Suddenly, a composite sketch flashed on the screen. I might have dropped my fork as I fumbled for the volume knob. Still, I don't believe that I heard a word coming from the set. I was transfixed by the sketch. At that moment, I knew what I wanted to do.

I started making calls the next day. It wasn't long before I was flying around the country, seeking out the best in the business to train and mentor me. Over the years, my reputation grew among local law enforcement as the phone calls came rolling in requesting my help. It was hard but satisfying work. Each capture bolstered my confidence, though it bothered me that someone had to be hurt or killed before I was called in for a sketch.

After thirty-one years in law enforcement in California, I retired as a police sergeant and began focusing on my sketching, consulting for law enforcement agencies throughout the country.

In 2011, I fulfilled a longtime career goal when I was hired as the Baltimore Police Department's first full-time forensic artist, the only one in the state of Maryland. Now it was time to put all that training and experience to work.

And there was lots of work to be done in Baltimore, one of America's most violent cities. I logged nearly 400 composite sketches during a three-year period. During that time, I tried to help as many victims as I could. I never said no to an investigator's request. I worked weekends and long shifts into the night, including middle of the night call-outs, just to keep up with the workload.

None of that bothered me, though. The victims and eyewitnesses were fascinating people, each with a unique story to tell. They ranged from street thugs to doctoral candidates. One was an opera singer and another a senior citizen who worked as a prostitute. Once, I was nearly choked out by a sexual assault victim re-enacting her attack, while another victim offered to sell me drugs during her composite sketch interview, to raise money for a bus ride to see her probation officer the following day.

Each day there was a new story that was more outrageous than the one before. There was no way you could make this stuff up. You couldn't help but feel sorry for some of the people. Many of them lived high-risk lifestyles, mired in poverty and drug abuse. All I could do for them as they moved through the criminal justice system was lend an ear and provide moral support, as we talked and I created a sketch that started them on their road to healing

When they passed through my doors to share their stories, I would offer them a cup of coffee and they would delight in trying to name the criminals depicted in caricatured posters that adorned the walls of my office. This became a great rapport-builder and helped jump-start many conversations.

One day, a crime victim who came to my office at the Baltimore Police Department for a sketch appointment asked if I ever became "bored" sitting in my office sketching all day long. I told her that my job was more about helping people than sketching. Each person that entered my office was special and had a unique story to tell. The art, I explained, was a tool to help the police. The final drawing became an illustration that accompanied a victim's story, much like those inside a book.

Even more important is the psychological first aid I provide to victims. It is important that they leave my office feeling empowered to move on with their lives. They can feel good about being involved in helping solve their case. Confronting their attacker again -- on paper -- is a powerful emotional moment that helps them begin the healing process.

Several years ago, someone asked me to explain what I did for a living. When I tried to sum up my career in simple words, it was still hard for them to understand. After seeing their confused expressions, I tried to think of a word that would be simple and direct. So I came up with the term "sketch cop." It wasn't long before, I became known as "The SketchCop," and the nickname stuck.

I don't know if the name will ever strike fear into the hearts of criminals. Wouldn't it be nice if it did? Either way, it has become the perfect description for what I do. And I remain forever thankful to the victims and eyewitnesses who trust sharing their most terrifying moments with me. It is not an easy thing for them to do, and it means a lot to me.

More than they will ever know.

MICHAEL W. STREED

Chapter 1
Killer Clowns

Staring at the clock, I watched anxiously as the time *approached three o'clock. Seconds dragged into minutes as the big hand on the clock inched slowly toward the top of the hour. In a few moments, the bell would ring, marking the end of another long school day.*

Typically, this was the time of day when we were content to sit quietly and wait patiently for our dismissal. But today was not your typical day. Today, things were different. Today, we were restless and frightened, ready to run for our lives.

As the time ticked down, we were perched nervously on the edge of our seats, bodies shifting, our weight leaning toward the door, hoping to be the first to run through it when the bell started ringing.

As the tension mounted, we began to swing our legs back and forth. With so many pairs of shoes scraping simultaneously across the smooth linoleum floor, it began to sound like a carpenter furiously rubbing sandpaper across pieces of rough-hewn lumber.

It wasn't long before nervous chatter replaced the sound of swinging feet. The sound of our voices rose steadily in volume until it drowned out the steady buzz from the tired old clock.

Finally, the bell sounded, plunging the school into total chaos. Without a moment of hesitation, we exploded from our seats. We tore through doors, into the narrow hallways. In seconds, we were everywhere, stampeding over the top of one another as we scurried toward any exit we could find, trying desperately to escape from school and flee to the safety of our homes.

Thundering footsteps rattled windows and shook frail nerves as we quickly fled the campus. And before the ancient timepiece stopped ringing, the last of hundreds of screaming children were barely a whisper in the distance as order was once again restored and a quiet calm returned to campus.

To understand the terror that led to the day's chaotic ending requires that you go back to the start of the school day. Like every day, it began innocently with the flag salute, followed by the principal's daily announcement, a mind-numbing blend of information he thought was important for us to know.

It became quickly apparent that today's announcement took on a far different tone than usual. The principal went off script to issue a warning about a man dressed in a clown costume loitering near the school. According to police, this clown had been spotted on several occasions attempting to lure children into his vehicle.

News of this clown touched off widespread anxiety. It wasn't long before "The Clown" was the topic of every conversation. All around the playground, children began to speculate about who would be his next victim.

Hushed whispers breathed life into a rumor that this clown was a killer. The realization that one of us could be plucked off the street, never to be seen again, dampened our nervous excitement, as the seriousness of the situation cast a pall across campus.

After the announcement, I spent the rest of the day moving about the campus, listening to the nervous chatter of my classmates. Their fearful comments made me wonder how things got out of control so quickly. No one ever said this clown was a killer. In my mind, he was nothing more than a harmless old man.

But funny or not, he was still out there. And until he was caught, this particular clown posed a danger to all of us.

To prove my feeling that this was just a silly clown, I decided to walk home alone. Things started out pretty well. With a clear patch ahead and no sign of The Clown, I was feeling good about my chances. That was, until I heard the sound of a slow-moving vehicle approaching me from behind. An uncomfortable feeling settled in as the engine noise grew louder, causing the ground to rumble beneath me. As the vehicle slowed to match my gait, my confidence began to crumble as I realized the vehicle and its occupant were stalking me.

It should have been obvious, but I had no clue about who would be following me. I stole a glance over my shoulder and was startled to see a dark-colored Ford Econoline van with a cheap set of whitewall tires keeping pace with each of my steps. The driver was a creepy-looking, older man. I struggled momentarily to figure out who he was and what made him look so weird. Was it the face painted shiny white, with bright colors circling his bloodshot eyes and darkened mouth? Or was it his red bulbous nose, littered with broken spider veins crawling across the bridge and blending into his ruddy cheeks. Whoever he was, his grotesque appearance made me shudder. I couldn't figure out why a clown would want to look so scary. Then it hit me -- it was The Clown!

I was suddenly paralyzed with fear. I didn't know what to do. Everything seemed so unreal. My first instinct was to run. But after quickly gauging the distance home, I realized *there was no way to make it there safely using the street. Shifting gears, I tried to think of alternatives.*

All I cared about was making it home. With absolutely no plan in mind, I decided it was now-or-never and broke into a dead run.

The Clown reacted by gunning his engine as he began to chase me. Several times he speeded up, jerking the steering wheel toward me, in an attempt to block my path. But each time he skidded to a stop, I leaped around the front of his van and kept running. Sensing an opportunity to finally get away, I hurtled over a low hedge and began zigzagging through several front yards.

The Clown ditched his van and began running after me. The sound of his feet pounding against the pavement was all I could hear. Or maybe, it was the sound of my own feet. At that point, it didn't really matter. The Clown was in hot pursuit, and I had to get away.

During the chase, I wanted to look back to see where he was. But I was afraid The Clown would reach out and grab me. When I finally looked, I was relieved to see that he was far behind. Around the time I began to feel good about my odds of escaping, a sprinkler tripped me up and sent me cartwheeling through the air. I hit the ground with a violent thud. The force of the impact scattered my books everywhere. I slowly rolled over to see The Clown smiling at me with crooked yellow teeth.

The Clown's breathing became labored and sounded like a death rattle. A few more yards probably would have killed him. He should have had a heart attack a couple of blocks back.

Slow to recover and unable to move, I now would be forced to surrender to his depravity. All I could do was lie there and wait.

As The Clown approached, I could smell the pungent odor

of cheap cologne. Mixed with the smell of stale cigarettes and whiskey from last night's drunk, The Clown reeked of death.

But I wasn't dead – yet.

In a last ditch effort to escape I tried to scoot backwards on the palms of my hands. Unfortunately, I wasn't fast enough. The Clown bent down to scoop me up in his dry, thick, tobacco-stained hands. As he lifted me off the ground, I turned my head away and winced in disgust at the smell of him.

I began screaming for help as loud as I could. All I wanted was for someone to rescue me. I knew that once The Clown carried me away, I would never be seen again. But no one was coming. I was all alone.

Suddenly, my screaming stopped as I woke and looked around. It was dark and difficult to see. It felt like I was in bed, but I couldn't be sure. My right hand began to search about, gliding across the sheets to reach for my wife. The place that was once hers was cold and empty. She had died several months before, and I had not yet gotten used to sleeping alone.

Soon, a calm feeling returned. I realized that my fear was nothing more than a bad dream and that I was safe at home. My eyes slowly closed as I slipped off to steal another hour of sleep. Thankfully, I wasn't trapped in the clutches of a killer clown, yet I lay aching from the emptiness one feels when they realize how truly alone they are.

As much as I tried, it was impossible to sleep. So I climbed out of bed to make my morning brew. It wasn't long before I was hunched over the morning edition of the Orange County Register enjoying a hot cup of coffee. My mind drifted away from the newspaper as I began thinking of The Clown. I began to replay the dream on a continuous loop inside my head, over and over again.

I couldn't help but think that my fear was unreasonable. Why after all these years would I have a nightmare about a clown? Weren't clowns supposed to be funny? I didn't really think so. Whenever I see a clown, it made me wonder about the kind of person who hides his face behind a semitransparent mask and plays with kids all day.

Maybe I felt that way because my first experience with a clown was that terrifying school day experience. To this day, I'm not really sure if he was ever identified or arrested. All I know is that this person cleverly used a clown costume as his "hook" to attract children. Luckily, I only encountered The Clown in a nightmare. Today I shudder just thinking about him. So I've spent my career thinking of ways to unmask the killer clowns of the world and sketch their hidden faces.

For the contemporary child molester, I think the lure of clown garb might be a bit over the top. Child molesters and killers have become more sophisticated in the methods they use to hunt their prey. With today's technology, it's become easier for them to identify and stalk their victims.

Luckily, the clown from that day at school, revived in my dream, disappeared without anyone getting hurt. The fear he left within me is something I still think about from time to time, yet I realize that brief terror is nothing compared to that experienced by children who have been abducted and later murdered.

Maybe that's the reason why for the past thirty-five years I've been drawn to use my skills in some of the country's most high-profile child abduction and murder cases. Cases like those of three-year-old Laura Bradbury, who disappeared in 1984 from a campground at Joshua Tree National Park in Morongo Valley, California, or Anthony Martinez, 10, taken from Beaumont, California, in 1997.

After them, there was Anna Palmer, age ten, sexually assaulted and killed in 1998 on her front porch in Salt Lake

City, Utah. And, in 2002, five-year-old Samantha Runnion, taken while playing by her apartment complex in Stanton, California, and later found dead.

These children and countless others have suffered unthinkable horrors at the hands of people society failed to protect them from. All are a grim reminder that there is still more work to be done. For them, I am committed to doing whatever is necessary.

I am grateful for the opportunity to lend my skills to dedicated investigators who work hard to bring these monsters to justice. Being a part of their team is one of the most rewarding aspects of my career.

For those of us in law enforcement, the search for justice begins in several different ways. For me, it began with a faceless man that I considered a killer clown, and it hasn't ended since.

It probably never will.

MICHAEL W. STREED

Chapter 2
FREEZE ... POLICE!

Thoughts wandered through my head as I thought of a phrase I'd shouted in frustration so many times over the years:

"FREEZE ... POLICE!"

I couldn't help but think what a useless phrase it was. I mean, what the hell? Nobody stops for the police anymore. These days, the only time I can get a crook to "freeze" is when their face is caught on my sketchpad.

It seems as though my pencil's become more useful to me than my gun. Over the years, I've been able to transform this simple little tool into a formidable weapon that rarely fails me. My pencil has helped me to use my skills in ways I never could have imagined. As a tool for law enforcement and a source of strength for those in suffering, it's been pointed in the direction of some of the worst crooks imaginable.

So, as my pencil gently scratched across the page that day, I got back to work and refocused on the task at hand. With childlike fascination, I watched as my rhythmic strokes began causing a form to take shape, the lines blending to create an evil visage, as the assailant's face began materializing before me.

Glancing up for a moment, I could see the victim staring wide-eyed at me. In her eyes, I saw a jumble of both fear and hope. Fear from the terror she experienced combined with hope that she would be able to hold the frightening image of her attacker in her mind's eye for just a moment longer.

The pressure was building to finish the task. But, why would I worry? Wasn't I "The SketchCop"? Wasn't it my pencil that became the magic bullet to make things happen?

I chuckled quietly as I thought to myself, "That impression couldn't be further from the truth."

That's because in most instances it's the hard-working street cop who makes the breaks and gets the job done. While my role is critical to many investigations, the process remains a team effort. I won't minimize my role, but I would never overstate it either.

Often I'm just a piece of the investigative puzzle. In many cases, I've helped make a difference, but there are many others out there too. They practice a wide range of forensic disciplines and are experts in their fields. They too deserve to share credit for the successful conclusion of a case.

Sometimes I've wondered, "Wasn't it easier just being a cop?"

The truth is, I've been a law enforcement professional for so many years, I have a hard time remembering when I wasn't a cop.

As long as I can remember, there was a uniformed presence in our household in Orange. There always seemed to be cops hanging around. You know the saying, "Why is there never a cop around when you need one?" That's because they were always hanging out over at our house!

I'd wake up in the morning, and there would be a detective having breakfast. When I went to bed at night or when I came home from school, it was a uniformed officer having a cup of coffee.

I would even share my holidays with them. Sounds weird doesn't it? It wouldn't be if your father were a cop. Mine was. Between him and his friends, our household pretty much looked like a Fraternal Order of Police Lodge.

From my earliest childhood memory, I can recall that when he was off at work, I was busy patrolling our neighborhood on my shiny blue three-wheeled police "motor-tricycle." Resplendent in my own uniform of the day, I was a four-year-old pint-sized badass in blue and ready for action!

I pointed my vehicle out of the driveway and pedaled up and down the street looking for the suspects of the day – cats.

Yes, CATS ... lots of them. The loathsome creatures seemed to be lurking everywhere! To rid the neighborhood of this scourge, I developed a plan to stalk them, corner them and arrest them. I figured that without them, the neighborhood would be a safer place. At least, so it seemed in the mind of a young child.

The truth was, all I cared about was impressing my parents with what a great cop I could be, just like Dad.

I had this cool set-up. It was police-style tricycle with a metal box mounted on back, its metal door clanging open and shut each time I pedaled over a crack in the sidewalk. At the time, it seemed like the perfect jail for my prey.

It wasn't long before I spotted my first cat. I watched as it quietly stalked its invisible prey around my front yard. My clumsy surveillance lasted only a moment though as I became impatient and sprang into action.

Cornering the cat, I grabbed it in a bear hug to carry it off to my makeshift jail. I stuffed it into the box on my tricycle and triumphantly pedaled into the driveway. Hearing the clanging of the door, I looked back to realize the cat had found an escape hatch and run for its life.

Frustrated but undeterred, I located him again later that morning. Like before, I grabbed him in what today is considered an unauthorized police control hold. Rather than risk another escape, I quickly walked him toward my house to take him to the ultimate judge ... my mom.

The cat, not wanting any part of me or my plan, began squirming about trying to wrestle himself free. This of course only strengthened my resolve, causing me to tighten my grip.

Suddenly, I felt something warm and moist running down the front of my shirt. I looked down as the cat began hissing and screaming while exacting his revenge. This, of course, caused me to start crying and screaming as I ran toward the safety of my house.

As I sat there sketching, the thought of all those screams sparked another memory, of a time when there was no safe place to hide when all the screaming started. That tactical staff sergeant at the police academy went nose-to-nose with me, hissing and screaming in my face louder than that darn cat! Damn, that guy could scream. And if you were unlucky, you might just get the entire tactical staff, one voice for each side of your head.

These guys loved playing an evil game of four-square on your psyche. I was pretty good, though, at deflecting the verbal abuse. With my personal background, I went into Golden West College's police academy in Huntington Beach knowing the whole thing was a game. But how long could I play it?

If words weren't enough, the tactical staff punished your body. They had this special place for us they called "The Blade," a large, hot, black square of unforgiving asphalt. This was the place where, in their words, they "honed us to a razor-sharp edge." Hidden on a corner of the campus away from the prying eyes of other students, we spent many hours there being "sharpened." I figured by the time they finished with us, we should have been able to split even the finest hair.

But, as an old police chief I once worked for so eloquently

stated, "the more you sweat here, the less you bleed out there." Thinking about what he said as I lay there sweating in the hot sun, I could only think to myself, "Tell that to my bleeding, blistered hands, you bastard."

I had stubbornly resisted my father's efforts to talk me out of becoming a cop. Normally I valued his wisdom and, like an obedient son, went along with his wishes. Now, as I was busy applying the finishing touches to a drawing, I thought to myself that I was glad I didn't listen -- because now, I'm The SketchCop.

The stories that I'm about to share with you are an anthology of events from my personal files detailing some of my more significant and challenging cases. Each was unique and required me to use my skills and experience to help solve them.

You'll also read about other dedicated professionals, each of whom worked hard to bring justice for those we serve.

After reading this book, it's my belief that you'll never look at a face the same way again. And who knows, you might even spot a couple of crooks!

MICHAEL W. STREED

Chapter 3
Fast Food, Slow Justice

Wailing sirens pierced the chill of a winter evening as officers raced toward a report of a robbery that had just occurred at a Burger King restaurant in Orange, California. As we raced toward the scene, our radios crackled with an update: There was now a "man down" inside the location.

Officer Larry Forrester, then a six-year police veteran and SWAT team member, was the first officer to arrive. As he pulled his patrol car to a stop in the front parking lot, he was confronted by several panicked restaurant employees. Forrester leaped from his vehicle to question the restaurant's crew, who were upset and confused by what had just happened.

Based on the dispatcher's radio updates, Forrester was wary that the gunman might still be inside the restaurant. To determine if he was, the officer asked the employees several times, "Is he gone?" But they just shouted back at him repeatedly, "They shot Walter!"

Initially, Forrester decided that he would wait for backup. Peeking through the front windows, he could see the back door standing open. Was it possible the suspect exited through that door? Or was he waiting inside to ambush police? Based on what he saw, Forrester couldn't really be sure.

One thing Forrester was sure of -- a critically wounded victim was inside the restaurant waiting for help. Weighing his options, he made the courageous decision to not wait for backup, but enter the restaurant to rescue the victim. He carefully made his way back to the office, where he found the night manager was dead.

As other officers began to arrive, Forrester returned outside where he was finally able to obtain the suspect's description from the horrified witnesses. He broadcast the description to the rest of us who were desperately waiting for the information as we circled the area in our cruisers hoping to locate a suspect.

Once the description was broadcast, we fanned out looking for the killer whom witnesses described as a black man in his mid-twenties, approximately 6-foot and 175 pounds with black hair wearing a "beanie-style cap" and a long, dark-colored jacket. While the rest of us searched, Forrester remained at the crime scene to help protect it from curious onlookers and to preserve any evidence that the suspect might have been left behind.

After an exhaustive and lengthy area search, it appeared as if the suspect had disappeared into the night. His take for his actions? Approximately $2,500 and the life of an innocent young man, someone he didn't know and had no reason to kill. Frustrated at our inability to find him, a few of us continued our search throughout the remainder of the shift as we fielded calls for service.

Thinking back to that shift and how the night of Dec. 11, 1980, began, I would describe it as pretty routine.

With other officers from the Orange Police Department, I was preparing for another busy graveyard shift. The patrol assignment began just before midnight and stretched into the morning hours, ending just about the time the sun was rising. Generally, it was a busy shift that saw its fair share of crime.

Each night, we gathered in the roll call room and anxiously waited for our sergeants to finish their nightly briefing so we could "hit the streets" and catch some crooks.

Once we peeled out of the station's parking lot, we spent the night roaming the city, sucking up crooks like human street sweepers. Our group was tight and efficient. Each night we challenged each other to lock up more crooks than the night before. We worked hard each and every shift, making sure the city was safe for citizens and unsafe for criminals.

Dwayne McKinney was a violent offender who had plenty of experience with "street sweeping" police. McKinney was an alleged member of the notorious Los Angeles-based Crips street gang and carried the nickname "Crazy Wayne." His criminal background included a variety of offenses such as assaulting and cutting a woman with a knife plus an attempted armed robbery involving a firearm.

McKinney's violent criminal history was in sharp contrast to a description by friends who said he was a kind and caring individual. One female acquaintance said that often times he bought food for her and her young child or would sometimes help pay her bills.

But, despite these acts of kindness, McKinney kept finding himself in jail. His last prison stint had ended three months before the murder in the restaurant in Orange.

McKinney, now a parolee, moved in with friends in their apartment in Ontario, about thirty miles east of Orange.

Although his friends tried keeping him out of trouble, McKinney still seemed to find it. A month before the Burger King shooting, McKinney was visiting Los Angeles when someone tried to kill him. During the attack, McKinney suffered a serious shotgun wound to his calf. The blast caused him to limp when he walked, first while using crutches and later a cane.

While McKinney was back in Ontario recovering from

his wounds, the Burger King workers were busy closing their restaurant for the night. As they were cleaning up, officers were streaming out of the back parking area of the Orange Police Department heading toward their assigned patrol beats.

Officer Forrester was assigned to work the area where the Burger King was located. Nestled on a darkened patch of West Chapman Avenue, between the Pomona Freeway and the Santa Ana River, the restaurant was a perfect robbery target. Forrester was aware of this and consistently began his shift by first driving through the darkened parking lot as he snaked his way westward toward the farthest-most areas of his patrol beat.

Tonight, though, Forrester was having equipment problems that slowed his departure from the police parking lot. This threw off his routine, and he was a couple of minutes late getting to the Burger King for his usual drive-through of the parking lot.

So while Forrester was heading west, the Burger King employees were scurrying about inside the restaurant, working hard to finish their cleaning duties so they could go home. The only thing that slowed them down that night was a broken front door lock. Unable to secure the restaurant, someone occasionally had to monitor the front entrance.

During one such status check, an employee was startled by a man who seemed to appear out of nowhere, acting like a customer. He was told the restaurant was closed and was offered a free soft drink for his trouble. But the stranger spurned the offer and quickly vaulted over the counter.

Witnesses later told police that the suspect easily jumped the forty-inch-high barrier at the same time he pulled out a handgun and announced the robbery. After landing on the other side, the suspect gathered the employees together and herded them into a large walk-in style cooler.

As they filed inside what could have been a cold, dark tomb, the gunman grabbed one of the employees by the back of his shirt collar and jerked him from the group. He pressed the tip of the gun barrel against the back of the employee's head and ordered him to lead him to the night manager's office. The employee tried telling the gunman that the manager was in the bathroom.

He knew this was a lie, but he was trying to save the popular night manager, Walter Horace Bell, who was busy counting cash and had no idea he was about to be robbed.

The gunman didn't believe his lie. He could see several cash drawers and paperwork strewn about through the doorway, so he knew that the manager was inside.

When they reached the office, the suspect confronted the nineteen-year-old Bell, who was seated at his desk. Fearing for his life, Bell followed directions and did exactly what he was told. There was no way he was going to be a hero, especially with a young wife at home, pregnant with their first child.

The gunman ordered the employee to lie face down on the floor. After Bell opened the safe, the gunman ordered him to remain seated at his desk, face down.

By this time, the gunman was becoming nervous and frustrated. He mumbled to himself as he quickly gathered the cash. He seemed to be having difficulty handling the gun and the money while simultaneously barking orders.

Now that he had the money and was preparing to leave, the suspect pointed his gun at the back of Bell's head and told him, "Don't move, or you'll get this."

As he issued that threat, witnesses reported hearing the gun discharge, and a .22 caliber bullet tore into the back of Bell's head, killing him instantly.

The police response to the employees' 911 call was swift. Forrester arrived within a minute. Several other units followed and were also there within moments of the initial call.

I wasn't quite as fast as the others were and spent my time in the surrounding areas conducting a search for the suspect. At the time, there was only a small African American population in Orange. So at that time of night, in that part of the city, it would be highly unusual to see any number of black men walking around. And, unfortunate as it sounds, any black man who was found in the area that night, who matched the suspect's description, would be closely scrutinized. Today, some would call this racial profiling, even though we were responding to a serious crime and acting on a genuine eyewitness description.

A couple of miles from the crime scene, I was driving southbound on Main Street, when I saw a tall African American man, sporting a medium Afro haircut, wearing jeans and a worn-looking camouflage jacket. He was moving with a carefree stride while carrying a dark gym bag. I watched for a moment as he neared the southern edge of the city. I considered his appearance, going down a mental checklist from the suspect description, and noted that there were too many similarities to ignore. He was about to cross into another jurisdiction, so I decided to act.

At the time I was making my observation, there were no backup officers available. I couldn't make it onto the radio to notify our dispatcher about my activity because of all the radio traffic about the robbery and shooting clogging the airwaves.

I wanted the element of surprise to be to my advantage, so I drove up quickly behind him, slammed on my brakes and leaped from my police car. I braced him against the hood of my car and restrained him by pinning him with my body weight as I took his bag. Inside, I felt a long hard object. A gun, maybe?

I stuck my hand inside and felt a pair of nunchuks, a martial arts striking weapon popularized by Bruce Lee in his movie "Enter the Dragon." A nunchuk is constructed with two hard, cylindrical pieces of wood, each about twelve inches long, connected by a short chain.

Anyone that has ever tried to use them would quickly learn how easy it is to hurt yourself with them if you aren't careful. And at the time, it was a felony to possess them in the state of California under certain conditions.

After a short conversation, I learned that the man was walking home from a friend's house, unaware of what had taken place at the Burger King.

Weighing whether or not I should have arrested him for a felony weapons violation, I decided to take a pass and let him go home. I didn't have time to arrest him anyway because I had a killer to catch. Besides, it was an innocent mistake on his part and we were both breathless after scaring the daylights out of each other. So I apologized to him for the inconvenience, took a deep breath and continued my area search.

Meanwhile, back at the restaurant, officers were busy securing the crime scene. It wasn't long before detectives and crime scene technicians began to arrive. Once there, detectives got down to business right away and talked to witnesses while crime scene personnel searched for clues that might identify the killer.

Detectives knew the community would react to the crime with shock and demand that it be solved quickly. Those who lived in Orange had become spoiled by years of low crime rates. They recognized it was the result of an aggressive police department that was supported by the community. This case was different from others, though, and would be difficult to solve as the only evidence left behind was a group of traumatized witnesses and a partial latent fingerprint.

Detectives would separate these witnesses and transport them to the police department for more detailed interviews. Keeping them separated would prove a challenge as the detectives' office, which they called The Bullpen, was nothing more than a long, open, rectangular room, littered with desks, with no partitions and little privacy.

With all the witnesses now corralled at the department, detectives were eager to get things rolling. They first wanted to produce a composite sketch for public release. They hoped the sketch would help generate solid leads that would point to a suspect, followed by a quick identification and arrest.

Detectives were aware that I had recently completed an introductory course in police composite drawing the year before while I was a deputy sheriff in Santa Barbara.

At the time of the Burger King shooting, I was relatively inexperienced. Up until that night, I had only worked on minor cases. But, for now, I was all they had, so I was called in from the field to develop a sketch.

Before I arrived, detectives processed a witness. I was introduced to him, and we quickly settled down in a private interview room so we could get to work. The witness turned out to be the young man who was inside the office when Bell was shot and killed. At the time of our interview, he was still nervous and upset. His emotional state was understandable, considering what he just experienced.

And now here he was, in a police station, sitting in front of a uniformed cop with a pencil, ready to interrogate him. Staring at him across a table that separated us, I am sure that I looked pretty menacing with my gun and badge prominently displayed. Back then, I was still pretty fresh on the job and didn't realize the negative effect my appearance could have on a cooperative witness. I thought the display of authority only scared crooks!

Luckily, despite our awkward start, the interview moved along. We worked together to flesh out the facial proportions and began developing the suspect's facial features. But some problems began to crop up because the witness was still upset. I spent more time trying to have him stay focused on what we were doing than I did drawing.

Sometime during the interview, and I am not really sure when, the eyewitness turned hostile toward me. He wasn't happy with the way the sketch was developing, and he let me know it.

As the interview wore on, he would change a facial feature, be satisfied with it, before becoming dissatisfied and demanding I change it back to what we had just changed. This went on for the better part of an hour. Finally, he told me that he could do no better, and we finished the sketch.

Thankfully, after all our hard work, he agreed that the sketch represented a good likeness of the gunman, so I turned the sketch over to detectives.

In retrospect, sometimes it is better for police to pursue other leads while allowing an eyewitness to go home to eat and sleep. I understand the need to get information out right away, but I think that you receive more cooperation and a more focused eyewitness when you show compassion and tend to their needs, even if it is for just a couple of hours. In this instance, it turned out that might have been a better strategy.

The following day, as detectives released the sketch to the media, pathologists were busy conducting the autopsy on Walter Bell.

They carefully examined Bell and found that the bullet entered the back of his head approximately two inches behind the right earlobe. The bullet's path destroyed Bell's cerebrum, his cerebellum and his brain stem. Doctors estimated the bullet was fired anywhere from eighteen to thirty-six inches away from Bell's head. Assuming that Bell was standing when the gun was fired, the bullet traveled in a slight, upward direction, right to left, from back to front.

With Bell's death now officially classified as a homicide, detectives continued their investigation. They talked to local law enforcement agencies who shared information with them that the Crips gang from Los Angeles had recently been involved in similar robberies throughout Orange County.

These same law enforcement agencies supplied detectives with a stack of photos representing known Crips members. Immediately after receiving them, detectives began to pore over them. One of the photos they found closely resembled my composite sketch. The name on the back of the photograph was Dwayne McKinney.

His photo was placed into a lineup with photographs of five similar-looking men, and the array was shown to eyewitnesses. After viewing the photographs, they told detectives they felt the nineteen-year-old McKinney most closely resembled the killer.

Author's sketch is on the left, McKinney's photo is on the right.

Six days after Bell's murder, detectives located and arrested McKinney outside his friend's apartment, and he was booked into the Orange County Jail on suspicion of robbery and murder.

Now, with McKinney in custody and steadfastly denying his involvement in the robbery and murder, prosecutors would have to build a solid case around nothing more than eyewitness identification and some pieces of circumstantial evidence.

The first step toward a conviction would require that detectives conduct a "live" line-up at the jail. The witnesses would stand behind one-way glass to view a gallery of suspects, including McKinney. Inside the small viewing room, they could see the suspect's entire physical appearance, how he walked, how he talked, as well as his posture while standing still. A positive identification would bolster their photo identification of McKinney and help strengthen the police case.

Peering through the one-way glass, the witnesses said they thought they saw "something familiar" in McKinney's eyes. They eventually told detectives that McKinney was the one they saw come into the restaurant and rob them, killing their friend.

Although there was nothing conclusive in the partial latent fingerprint that pointed to McKinney, the eyewitness identifications were enough to convince the District Attorney's Office to file murder charges. With the police investigation completed, it was up to prosecutors to continue pursuing the case and take it to trial.

The Criminal Trial

With the case moving through the courts, prosecutors and defense lawyers were busy preparing for trial. As they reviewed police reports and eyewitness statements, I began receiving telephone calls from the Orange County Public Defender's Office wanting to talk to me about the sketch.

It seemed that their investigators had re-interviewed the eyewitness who helped me create the sketch. They learned about our "contentious" interview and his apparent unhappiness with the results. Now they wanted to talk to me to see what I would have to say about it. But there was really nothing I wanted to say to them, or would say to them, other than what I would testify to at trial.

The trial began with prosecutors focused on the eyewitnesses' identification.

On the other side, the defense immediately tried to undercut prosecutors by creating reasonable doubt. They attacked the eyewitness testimony as being a case of mistaken identity. Even though, during the trial, three of the witnesses were "sure" McKinney was the gunman while the fourth was unsure, stating that he "thought" McKinney might be the one.

The eyewitness description of the gunman's height also became an issue. On the night of the murder, eyewitnesses described the killer as being from 6-foot-1 to 6-foot-3, while McKinney was only 5-foot-9½.

Other reasons that McKinney might have been unable to commit the robbery soon were raised, primarily that he had a gunshot wound to his right calf at the time the crime was committed but witnesses said he jumped over the counter with ease.

During the trial, the Ontario Police Department officer who arrested McKinney, six days after the slaying, testified that he walked with a limp.

Regardless of what the defense had to say, the eyewitness identification evidence was compelling. In an attempt to further weaken the identifications, McKinney's lawyer argued that the Orange police detective who investigated the case had allegedly made prejudicial statements before the in-person lineup. The detective was reported to have told witnesses they had arrested someone in connection with the murder and had found a significant amount of money and matching clothing inside the car.

Earlier court rulings are clear that police are not allowed to comment to witnesses about any arrests or evidence found, no matter if that's based in truth or lies. In response to defense allegations, the detective denied making the comments.

Other evidence introduced by prosecutors included three .22 caliber bullets found inside a nightstand drawer next to McKinney's bed and a car he bought in the days following the murder for $575, using small bills, all of which was circumstantial evidence.

And although the bullets were similar, they were not the same brand used to kill Bell. Regarding the car, McKinney's girlfriend testified that he had told her three completely different stories about where the money to buy it came from – the first was gambling proceeds, the second was a loan from a friend, while the third was that his brother gave the money to him.

When it was time for McKinney's defense to make its case, he testified on his own behalf, telling the jury that the money had come from his brother, who was a convicted armed robber.

Defense lawyers then attacked my sketch as being unreliable on the grounds that it wasn't based on the witness's memory. They alleged that I refused to make the changes in the sketch the witness asked for and therefore was not a valid likeness of their client.

Later, the eyewitnesses were also attacked on the stand and, like me, withstood a barrage of hostile questions.

After both sides presented their cases, it was time for

lawyers to sum things up and make final arguments to the jury.

Orange County Deputy District Attorney Anthony "Tony" Rackauckas spoke for the prosecution. In his closing statement, Rackauckas argued that evidence in the case was overwhelming. He told jurors that the only logical conclusion to reach was that McKinney was guilty of murder. He told the jury that the only better piece of evidence would be "if they had a movie of the crime."

Orange County Deputy Public Defender Christopher Strople represented McKinney. Strople made a passionate argument that McKinney's prosecution was the result of racial bias that was influenced by the county's majority white population.

After considering their arguments, the jury returned a guilty verdict against McKinney for murder in the shooting of Walter Horace Bell.

With the guilt phase now complete, it was time for the penalty phase, during which jurors would be asked to impose the death penalty. But, after careful deliberation, jurors were unable to return a decision. They told the judge that they remained hopelessly deadlocked with seven jurors voting for the death penalty and five voting against it.

With the jury unable to decide his punishment, McKinney's sentence was allowed by law to automatically revert to life in prison.

While many now considered the trial completed, information regarding alleged jury misconduct was beginning to surface. These allegations led to McKinney being retried for the penalty phase of his previous trial. In the end, the results remained the same. He was again found guilty of murder and sentenced to life in prison.

McKinney, who still declared his innocence, had heard something during the trial that gave him hope. He was being held in the Orange County Jail, where he met another prisoner who claimed he knew the identity of the "real" killer. The prisoner told McKinney that he helped plan the robbery and that his cousin drove the getaway car. McKinney passed the information along to his attorneys hoping it would lead to his exoneration and release from jail. But the information was never acted upon, and McKinney went to prison.

Prison Life

McKinney was transferred from the jail to a California state prison to begin serving his life sentence. Without the possibility of parole, he would have plenty of time to mount other appeals or to try to prove his innocence. For now, that would all have to wait.

McKinney's main focus now was survival. He had already survived a stabbing inside an Orange County holding cell while awaiting trial, and soon he was stabbed again inside the prison. To help survive future attacks, McKinney would fasten several magazines around his chest to act as a protective layer, much like a bulletproof vest.

Protective measures were especially important for him because he was housed in a cellblock alongside other Crips gang members who were targeted by the Mexican Mafia, a rival prison gang.

Before long, the pressure of prison life became too much for him. McKinney attempted suicide by cutting his wrist. Much to his relief, he was removed from the notorious cellblock until his wounds healed. McKinney's relief was short-lived, however, as he then was returned to his old cell.

The worst part about prison was that McKinney felt as if those close to him had forgotten him. In prison, his only link to the outside world was the mother of his young child.

After much soul searching, he decided it would be better

for her, and his son, if she moved on with her life. During a heartbreaking conversation, he told her to go out and find someone to marry who could become a father figure to the boy.

Honoring his wishes, she met another man and married. Soon after, she stopped bringing their son to prison to visit McKinney.

Enduring what McKinney experienced during his prison odyssey, many would have become embittered. McKinney decided to choose a different path and became spiritually renewed. Regular visits from religious outreach groups helped lift his spirits and provided him new hope.

Prison-based religious conversions become highly suspect because inmates can use them as a tool to demonstrate remorse and redemption for their crimes. This can mislead prison officials and parole boards into releasing a violent prisoner who really deserved to stay locked up.

McKinney's case was different. His religious experience seemed genuine. Due to the severity of the charges and strict sentencing guidelines, he would not be released, so there was no reason to suspect his religious conversion.

For the next few years, he depended upon his faith to help buoy him as he continued to hold out hope that he would one day be released.

It wasn't until 1997, nearly twenty years after Bell's murder, that McKinney's hope was renewed when he ran into the same inmate who years earlier had claimed to have knowledge about the real killer.

The inmate's name was Charles Hill. For years, he held a secret that would become key to McKinney's eventual exoneration. Wracked by guilt, he told McKinney the full story of the night of Bell's murder. After hearing Hill's story, McKinney urged him to write a letter to the Orange County Public Defender's Office. McKinney instructed him to detail his participation in the crime and what he knew about the suspect. Hill agreed and penned the letter, taking the extraordinary step of having it notarized prior to sending it.

The letter sent a jolt through the Orange County Public Defender's Office. The information created an opportunity for the defense attorneys to open an investigation into Hill's allegations. Finally, they believed they held the key that would open the door and free Dwayne McKinney.

The letter detailed how three people -- Hill, his cousin Willie Charles Walker and Raymond Hermann Jackett III -- had planned the robbery at the home of Hill's aunt.

During the meeting, Jackett asked permission to use Hill's .45 caliber handgun. Jackett said that his own .22 caliber handgun wasn't "working right" and would "only fire sometimes."

Hill refused to let Jackett use his gun. He told Jackett that he shouldn't even be thinking about shooting anyone. After Jackett's request, he became worried about the man's true intentions. Hill was aware Jackett had violent tendencies, and he did not want to be part of a robbery where someone might be killed. So Hill backed out.

After they received the letter, investigators from the Public Defender's Office contacted Walker. He admitted to his participation as the getaway driver and named Jackett as the shooter. He told investigators that on the night of the murder, he parked alongside the Pomona Freeway and Jackett went inside to rob the restaurant. Moments later, Walker heard a gunshot and saw Jackett run out the back door carrying a gun in one hand and a bag in the other.

To further prove his knowledge of the details, Walker sketched a detailed map for investigators. His sketch showed an overview of the area, including the Burger King restaurant and the parking lot surrounding it.

Interviews with Walker's relatives revealed that he had

told them in 1981 about Jackett committing the murder. Hill also told investigators that he was present when Walker and Jackett returned from the robbery and divided the money among the group and talked about the shooting.

Authorities would later question why the allegations would surface after so many years had passed. What would their motivation be? The men didn't know McKinney, and they surely didn't owe him anything.

Hill and Walker had later been convicted of a series of rapes and robberies that were unrelated to the 1980 murder case. Hill was sent to prison where encountered Jackett's brother, who threatened him and told Hill to keep his mouth shut about Bell's murder. Hill was reluctant to testify against his cousin, Walker, and be branded a "snitch." If Hill testified, he would surely have problems in prison, especially if it got him a shortened sentence.

Public Defender's Office investigators dug further and learned that Jackett was serving a prison sentence for drug possession and welfare fraud. He was scheduled for release in the next couple of years. Investigators obtained photos of Jackett and again contacted the witnesses who had identified McKinney and testified against him.

In what some decried as a questionable investigative tactic, investigators told the witnesses they had recently uncovered information about the "real" killer. They showed the witnesses photos of Jackett, along with a second sketch that I had done on the night of the slaying and long ago forgotten.

This sketch was definitely different from the one that resembled McKinney's comparison photo. The facial features were slightly different, and the person illustrated had tufts of hair sticking out from under the beanie cap indicating a longer hairstyle.

The information illustrated in the sketch was consistent

with a mugshot of Jackett from a previous arrest. In that photo, he wore his hair in a long Afro. McKinney wore his closely cropped.

The second sketch of Jackett was never publicized. Considering McKinney's and Jackett's physical differences and the appearance of the suspect in the second sketch, it certainly called McKinney's identification into doubt.

After viewing Jackett's photo, two of the witnesses now expressed doubt about McKinney's guilt and said they felt that Jackett more closely resembled the person who robbed them and shot Bell. Their change of heart would create reasonable doubt about McKinney's guilt but also could possibly hinder further prosecution of Jackett due to the way the identification had been made.

Denise Gragg, an assistant public defender and ardent death penalty foe, had taken up McKinney's case. Gragg, described by her colleagues as fair and intelligent, was dedicated to her clients and passionate in their defense.

The information provided by her investigators was used in her writ of habeas corpus asking the court to free McKinney based on the new information.

In legal documents asking for McKinney's release, Gragg also cited many examples of errors allegedly committed by the courts and police while prosecuting McKinney. They included mistaken identity, alleged police misconduct, alleged jury misconduct and alibi witnesses provided by McKinney.

Gragg was stunned when a judge approved her writ and ordered McKinney's release, prompting the District Attorney's Office to launch its own investigation.

After the District Attorney's Office investigation was completed, the conclusion was that McKinney was not involved in the 1980 robbery and slaying at the Burger King restaurant and instead was probably at home with friends as he initially had told police.

Tony Rackauckas, now the elected district attorney for Orange County, courageously followed his investigator's recommendation that McKinney be freed. Although he had fought to take McKinney's life back in 1982, he was now in the position to make things right.

Many people praised Rackauckas' fairness and professionalism. He could have appealed the judge's ruling and left McKinney to languish in prison for several more years while his case wound through the system.

In the end, McKinney's long road to justice had become a path littered with mistakes that occurred despite the system's best intentions. Eventually, the mistakes were corrected. It was unfortunate that it took so long for someone to recognize.

Release From Prison

Most expected McKinney to come out and blast a legal system that pretty much stole away half his life. Instead, they found a warm, forgiving individual who was only interested in reclaiming his life and moving forward.

After McKinney was released, it seemed to him that the world had passed him by. He marveled at new technology like cellphones, microwave ovens and self-serve drink machines. He was also amazed at the lumbering traffic that now choked intersections and blocked roadways.

The experience of trying to take in all the sights, sounds and smells overwhelmed him. McKinney had told others that sometimes he felt sure this was all a dream and he feared that he would soon awaken, only to find himself back inside his prison cell.

But it wasn't a dream. McKinney was truly a free man. After his release, McKinney lived with his spiritual adviser as he readjusted to life outside of prison walls.

Back at the Public Defender's Office, the feeling was pure joy. This was the first case of its kind in the office's history and re-affirmed the attorneys' commitment to fight for the innocent.

Defending suspected criminals is not often a popular cause, but it is a right afforded to all of us by the U.S. Constitution. It is a critical part of the checks and balance of our legal system. In addition, I think if any of us felt wrongly accused, the first phone call we would make would be to a good defense attorney.

In all fairness, the District Attorney's Office could be equally as proud. They showed compassion and fairness to a man they prosecuted with the best evidence they had at the time.

McKinney's case was one that came full circle, beginning and ending with the same career prosecutor who had the rare opportunity to free the man he had recommended be put to death.

McKinney went on later to become a popular speaker on the Christian lecture circuit. Wherever he went, he received a hero's welcome. Offers of money, housing and jobs soon came pouring in as his humility and positive attitude continued to impress people.

Many saw him as a man who had every reason to come out and condemn the system and those responsible for his imprisonment. However, instead, he said that being in jail probably saved his life, considering the road he was heading down before all that had happened.

As McKinney's life began to quiet down, he was able to pick up the pieces of his broken life by reconnecting with his estranged son. McKinney also married and later became a grandfather.

Lawsuits would soon follow as everyone tried to spread the blame. McKinney would receive money from the state for his wrongful imprisonment as well as settling other lawsuits with Orange County and the City of Orange.

Maybe if detectives and prosecutors had known earlier about Jackett, things would have turned out differently. They could have investigated his involvement and possibly freed McKinney years earlier.

Legal scholars believe that officials will never be able to charge Jackett with murder in the case due to the length of time that had passed and the effect on eyewitnesses' memories. Not to mention the questionable manner in which the Public Defender's Office conducted the photo identifications of Jackett.

Also, many witnesses had since tried to move on with their lives and were reluctant to become involved again for a variety of reasons. Convincing a jury to convict someone else after another man had been tried for the crime and then released on a prosecutorial error would also make it difficult to prosecute Jackett.

McKinney's case and several others since then have left many to question if we should continue sentencing people to death based only upon eyewitness identification. It's a tough question, and I can certainly see both sides of the argument. But if there is one thing I am certain of, it's that law enforcement agencies should use every tool at their disposal to ensure justice for crime victims and be quick to admit and correct mistakes they make.

Most of the time, the system and those of us within it get things right. When we don't, it's up to us to take an honest look at where we went wrong and work hard to make sure the same mistake doesn't happen again. That is why I am committed to always working hard to improve my methods and skills to better serve the victims I meet.

And what happened to McKinney?

He took his settlement money and moved to Hawaii,

where he invested in a string of automated teller machines and became a millionaire. With an oceanfront home and a bright future ahead of him, McKinney was killed in an accident while riding his moped on the island.

Reflecting back on this case, I believe it had elements we could all learn from. I think the best lesson was McKinney's display of grace and forgiveness. I am only sorry that he didn't get to fully enjoy making up for time lost.

Since the Bell murder case, I have gained a greater appreciation for the trauma people suffer as witnesses to violent crime. How I conduct eyewitness interviews today is much different from thirty-five years ago. This was the first high-profile crime in which I was asked to contribute my drawing skills. There was much pressure for me to perform. I think I did well under the circumstances, but it's foolish to ignore the value of well-developed communications skills to the creation of an accurate sketch.

Over time, developing myself into a skilled communicator has become my greatest asset. It is key to my successes during cases detailed in later chapters.

Don't get me wrong, being a good artist helps too. But absent the ability to obtain the information from your eyewitness, you might as well be drawing portraits down on the boardwalk.

For me, it's about helping victims. It always has been and always will be.

MICHAEL W. STREED

Chapter 4
Lines and Shadows

People often ask me how I am able to come up with such accurate sketches of crooks, time and time again. Sometimes, it's hard to explain. The process is driven by your victim or eyewitness and depends wholly on how well you are able to connect with them.

If you think it is easy, take a moment to think about how terrifying and difficult it could be to experience a crime and describe it later.

For example, let's say that late one evening you find yourself walking down a quiet, darkened street. Suddenly, you think you hear the sound of footsteps and feel that someone is walking up behind you. You stop and turn to look back, but no one is there.

Exhaling a sigh of relief, you feel yourself breathing heavily for no reason. Before long, your breath comes out in short bursts, soft and warm, like the gentle breeze that swirls around you.

Walking along with a heightened state of awareness, you listen closely to the sounds around you.

You can clearly hear the sound of leaves scraping as they're blown across the sidewalk in front of you. Though your confidence is shaken, you dismiss the previous noises while you continue walking, shrouded in fear.

You hear the scraping noises again. This time, though, they are louder and coming faster. Now you realize it's not the scraping of leaves in the wind, but someone running up behind you!

You react by walking faster. Turning to look over your shoulder, you capture a glimpse of the shadowy figure that's now upon you.

In the darkness, you see the steely flash of a gun or knife as a man brandishes his weapon. You freeze and listen intently, careful to hear each spoken word. And even though you don't really comprehend what he is saying, you automatically comply with his demands and give him everything you have.

The emotion that washes over you is a paralyzing wave of fear. You begin to pray that you won't be killed when, after what seems like an eternity passing, he's gone.

It's not until your fear subsides that you realize you've just been robbed and now -- you're a victim!

For some, the memory of such terror lasts a short time, for others a lifetime. Some never recover but are able to manage their trauma. But, in each case, there's a haunting face that they see in their mind's eye over and over again. Their ability to retrieve these lines and shadows and assemble them into a likeness of their assailant's face is key to a successful identification.

For the police sketch artist recovering the details in their memory can be a perilous, yet essential task. In the end, it doesn't really matter if the artist uses a pencil or computer to produce an image, because it is always the victim or eyewitness who provides the key information that is needed to successfully create a composite image.

That is because locked inside each person's memory are coded images from which facial features begin to emerge.

A police sketch artist's ability to mine this information successfully and use it to develop a sketch is critical during criminal investigations, especially when your only evidence is an eyewitness's description.

Probing the minds of victims and eyewitnesses is a delicate balance of pop psychology and modern-day criminology. Failing to properly connect and communicate with these important individuals can bring disastrous results to an investigation.

If not handled properly, a botched interview also can foster an atmosphere of mistrust and risk further trauma to your victim.

Keeping them engaged as an important element of the investigation can greatly assist with the end goal, which is the identification and successful prosecution of the suspect.

Although it may sound easy to some, it's not. Delving into someone's fragile psyche as you tiptoe past the trauma can be a delicate task that must be approached with care.

Sometimes it becomes a little more complex than just sitting down and talking to them. It's hard work, yet it can be satisfying. I can remember leaving many interviews physically and emotionally exhausted. It's the type of work that demands all of your personal resources.

That's because each eyewitness is different. I rarely interview the same eyewitness in the same way twice. Other situations create additional challenges the police sketch artist must overcome.

Human memory is tricky and is repeatedly challenged in court by defense attorneys and academics who are subject-matter experts. They consistently describe human memory as malleable and fatally flawed.

Their argument has been bolstered by recent advances in DNA technology, which has helped exonerate dozens of people, most of them who were sent to prison solely on the testimony of an eyewitness.

But despite these findings, eyewitnesses do get it right in many cases. They have come forward in cases to share their stories with police and prosecutors and have proven to be amazingly accurate in both their recollection of events and their identification of suspects.

That alone makes it worthwhile for investigators to continue using eyewitnesses to help develop composite images during their investigations.

The process of retrieving their memories and capturing them on paper goes to the heart of what we do as police sketch artists. Detectives rely on us to be skilled interviewers and apply our experience and techniques gleaned from the work of memory researchers at respected universities.

Most people are intrigued by how we develop a composite image, especially when one leads to an arrest. People are fascinated and believe the process is a closely guarded secret cloaked in mystery. As I stated at the beginning of the chapter, the most often-asked question is, "How do you do that?"

First of all, there's no mystery at all. The successful conclusion of a case begins and ends with the interview. The interview process defines our individual style and is the part of what we do that is both unique and personal to each of us. Of course, having strong drawing skills helps too.

To begin, the information we receive is translated by hand onto paper. To be successful requires you to be an active listener. It is essential that you make a quick and strong connection with the person you are interviewing.

In addition to being a successful interviewer, the police sketch artist must not be overly concerned about the final appearance of his or her sketch in regards to its aesthetic value. In other words, the police sketch artist must not become "ego-invested" while constructing the image.

Those who view a police sketch must keep in mind that it is not a posed portrait or the representation of an attractive, symmetrical face. Sometimes the resulting image looks unusual because these faces are drawn from the perspective of the eyewitness.

This can be a difficult concept for police investigators or others to understand. That is why it is important to keep in mind that the end result, regardless how attractive or unattractive, is nothing more than a piece of evidence, pure and simple. Even if it is not a strong resemblance to the suspect, as long as someone saw something in the image that resonated with him or her, then the composite image did its job.

An illustration of this is a case when detectives asked me to sketch a "window peeper" who was seen lurking outside a teenage girl's bedroom window.

She had been getting dressed for school early one morning when she heard a noise from the front yard planter, outside her bedroom window. She looked up and saw a man peering through the glass. Upon making eye contact with her, he realized he'd better hustle out of there and was gone before the first officer responded to the call.

The problem in this instance was that the victim only saw the upper portion of the suspect's face, from a point just below his eyes. The detectives were anxious for a drawing, so I completed a sketch of as much as she had seen, complete with a simulated window ledge just below his eyes. It's important to note that, in this case, the suspect had a distinctive hairstyle.

Naturally, everyone at the precinct got a great laugh from the sketch. For the next couple of days when I walked up to someone to say hello, the person would shield their lower face with a piece of folded, white paper, imitating my sketch. They would politely return my hello as they walked away laughing.

Within a few days, a patrol officer had identified a possible suspect with a similarly distinctive hairstyle near the victim's residence. He photographed the suspect in the field and forwarded the photo and his identifying information to detectives.

The hairstyle was dead on, and there was a great resemblance in the upper face as well. Although the man was not charged with a crime, the prowling activity in the neighborhood ceased after detectives interviewed him.

No one was laughing at my sketches after that. I think detectives learned the value of having even a partial sketch and realized why we only draw what an eyewitness sees.

I did not have any problems with the good-natured ribbing because I understand cop humor. But victims and eyewitnesses are courageous people who should always be handled with care. In many cases, they want to help, but we must never forget they're also human. So, while I use humor in many of my interviews, I never poke fun at them.

I have found that victims and eyewitnesses are motivated to tell the truth and help to the best extent their memory will allow. However, in some instances I have worked with people who have been less than truthful. Luckily, we have been able to detect their deception during our interviews before a case could go too far awry. This is when I use my intuition and experience to alert me when something's amiss. Otherwise, I have to rely on the detective to determine if the eyewitness is being truthful before they even get in front of me.

But some investigations are high-profile in nature and information develops quickly. Time becomes critical, and you don't always have the time to do proper fact checking beforehand. Many times, it's the interviews by the police sketch artist that yield new, critical information that investigators find helpful.

In October 1999, I was called by Riverside County sheriff's homicide investigators. A patrol deputy from their Jurupa Valley Sheriff's Station responded to a reported home invasion robbery. Within moments of arriving, the deputy was shot and killed by the intruder.

The armed suspect fled the scene and hid inside the brush of a nearby dry creek bed. Back-up officers who responded to the scene located the suspect. After refusing repeated commands to surrender, the suspect was shot and killed by arresting officers.

Over the next couple of hours, detectives received conflicting information about the number of suspects involved. Information provided by the robbery victim indicated there were two suspects. The elderly Hispanic woman reported that she had been tied up by the armed suspects, who took valuables from her home and were fleeing when they encountered the first deputy.

With one suspect now dead, the search focused on identifying and locating the second suspect.

Detectives requested that I meet with the victim inside her home to create a sketch of the second suspect. I began the interview aided by a Spanish interpreter. The victim was pleasant but seemed bored and disinterested with the process. She almost seemed detached, which is not uncommon behavior exhibited by someone suffering through a high-trauma event.

During the interview, each time I sketched a feature and shared it with her, she would just shrug her shoulders and simply say, "*Mas o menos*," which translated to English meant, "More or less."

The interview seemed too easy to me. There was little engagement by the victim. Initially, I thought it could be due to the language barrier. At the conclusion of the interview, we developed a generic-looking sketch that could have been mistaken for anyone.

Afterward, I shared my concerns with detectives. I recommended they not release the sketch to the public without further investigation. I just felt that something wasn't right. Her recollection came too easily and seemed a little too convenient.

I learned later that my suspicions were correct. There was no "they" only a "he." The suspect killed by deputies was her grandson, but she didn't identify him as a family member. The woman had no idea at the time of the interview that he was dead. It was my opinion that she fabricated the report of a second suspect to provide her grandson with the opportunity to escape.

Some people aren't creative enough to pull a face out of thin air and effectively describe it to a police sketch artist. In instances where an eyewitness is being less than truthful, the person fabricating a suspect for a police sketch is likely to describe a friend or maybe even the artist himself. I have to say, though, that describing a friend only works in instances when the police sketch artist doesn't know the friend being described.

In 1984, I was summoned to a local hospital by detectives from the Anaheim Police Department on a report that a uniformed security guard working at the Disneyland Resort had been shot in their guest parking lot. Luckily, the bullet struck him in the torso and his life was spared because of protective body armor he wore in violation of Disney's corporate policy. I knew the guard personally and had socialized with him on many occasions. After completing the drawing based on his description, I noticed it resembled an Orange police officer with whom I'd worked.

He was a beat partner of mine, and he also happened to be the victim's roommate. I immediately made the connection and alerted detectives.

It turned out the guard had fabricated the report after shooting and injuring himself at home, as well as damaging the body armor. He then wore the body armor to work so that when he reported a shooting at that location, it would be authenticated by the visible damage to the vest and his gunshot wound.

It turned out he went to such an extreme effort to call attention to security issues he felt strongly about and to improve his status with his peers.

His roommate knew nothing about the incident and was not amused that his likeness had turned up in the police sketch.

In other instances, victims have fabricated incidents and fictitious suspects as a way of taking focus off their own behavior. Children who are in trouble at school or late coming home may report an attempted kidnapping. A cheating spouse may report a sexual assault. Others may try to create a diversion to steer the focus away from their own behavior in an attempt to cover up crimes they've committed. With training, we are able to quickly recognize such deceptive behavior and turn our focus back to the truthful victims who need our help.

So, how does a police sketch artist tell when the eyewitness IS being truthful? In my experience, a strong physiological response by the eyewitness is a good indicator. Body language is another strong indicator, but it is not an absolute. Like anything else, all of our observations must be considered within the "totality of circumstances." In other words, all things must be considered.

An example of a strong physiological response occurred when I was working on a sketch with the victim of a vicious home invasion and sexual assault in the city of Corona. The suspect had used a ruse to gain entry to a residence. Once inside, he produced a handgun and fired a bullet into the ceiling. The victim, a middle-aged woman in her early forties, was terrified.

After raping the woman, he stole her vehicle. It was found abandoned a short time later in Lake Elsinore, approximately fifteen miles south of her home.

I interviewed her at her home. At the conclusion of our interview, I showed her the finished sketch. She began trembling violently and pushed the sketch away, running to another room where I could hear her vomiting. In my experience, a powerful physical reaction like that means a successful sketch.

Detectives later took the sketch to the neighborhood where the vehicle was abandoned and began contacting area residents.

During a visit to one home, they spoke to a resident who denied knowing anyone resembling the sketch. His young son came to the door and peeked at the sketch while his father talked to detectives. After seeing the sketch, the young boy blurted out, "That looks like my Uncle Tommy!"

Detectives were able to determine that "Uncle Tommy" was the suspect they were looking for. He strongly resembled the sketch, and the victim was able to successfully identify him.

Another example of a high-trauma case occurred a few years later when I was assisting the Long Beach Police Department during a carjacking/rape investigation.

A twenty-two-year-old college student was driving home alone one night. When she stopped at a red traffic signal, a man forced his way into her car and drove her to a remote location, where he raped her.

She agreed to help develop a sketch and brought her mother with her to police headquarters for support because she was still very frightened. I was not surprised at that, because it is important for victims of violent sexual assaults to have support people around them through the investigation and later court proceedings.

She was visibly upset, but seemed like a strong person as she sat beside her mother during much of the interview.

While I was busy refining the drawing for her to see, I looked up and saw that she had crawled up onto her mother's lap. Her mother was now cradling the young woman in her arms as if she were still a baby.

I looked at them and remember thinking to myself, "Great, now what am I supposed to do?"

I remained calm and in control as I ignored her near childlike state. I spoke to her quietly and calmly, coaxing her out of her mother's lap and bringing her back into the interview. By the time we completed the sketch, she was composed again.

By not visibly reacting to her behavior, I allowed her to retain her dignity. The results were positive. Police later arrested a suspect who strongly resembled her sketch.

Most witnesses we deal with on a daily basis, those known as "passive" witnesses, don't suffer the same depth of trauma. As witnesses who don't realize the significance of what they saw until later, they can be good witnesses. Conversely, without any emotional stake in the crime, they might not imprint facial details as well as someone suffering some kind of trauma.

Out of all the witnesses I have ever interviewed, some of the best ones were children. Their statements are pure, simple and uncluttered by the biases adults develop over the course of their lives. I've had several successes with kids as witnesses. Despite the justice system's reluctance to believe children can be reliable witnesses, I believe their testimony should be strongly considered when weighing the merits of using them during a criminal case.

To create a sketch that gets the strong responses I described, it is important to understand how memory works.

Memory occurs in three basic phases: storing, encoding and retrieval.

We make many observations daily using a variety of our senses, including vision, taste, hearing, touch and smell. Our brain processes these observations and determines their importance and relevance as it stores the information in the appropriate part of the brain. Think of your brain like a file cabinet at your home or office. You take paperwork daily and place it into folders for later retrieval. You file these folders based on their relevance and importance so if someone asks you for a report, you can retrieve it immediately. To accomplish the described task, you must first store them in the appropriate drawer so you can come back later and retrieve them as needed.

That last phase I described, the retrieval phase, is the most important to a police sketch artist. We know a particular event has been catalogued and stored. The ability to access it and properly record it now becomes key.

Outside influences and barriers affect our memory and our ability to access and retrieve vital information. Things such as lighting, distance, angle and time of observation can later affect how we perceive the landscape of a person's face. This would include details such as the spacing between the eyes or whether the person had a large nose or a small mouth.

In addition to the natural limits of memory, later recall can be affected by drug and alcohol abuse, as well as use of legal prescriptions.

When you see a police sketch, those are some of the things the artist takes into consideration when speaking with an eyewitness.

Recent high-profile cases in which suspect sketches have

been used successfully have created high expectations for continuing positive results.

Remember, a police sketch is no more than a graphic representation of a person's basic facial characteristics. A higher degree of detail, achieved through a skilled and practiced method of interviewing, can lead to a quicker identification.

The police sketch is designed to help police narrow their field of suspects. Even if the sketch artist can't create a highly detailed drawing, one that captures a prominent feature or provides a general overall likeness can be equally successful.

In developing a successful sketch, the artist must maximize the recognition skills of the witness. Studies have shown a person's ability to recognize someone is stronger than their ability to describe them verbally. When I am working with an eyewitness, I exploit both of these important components of human memory.

Retrieval of memories works best when a person is relaxed. Coming to the police station is never comfortable for anybody, least of all to anybody involved in a criminal investigation. I prefer it though, because I have much better control over the interview and the environment in which it's conducted.

Investigators conducting interviews for the purposes of producing a sketch, either mechanically assembled or drawn by hand, must remember to interview, not interrogate. There is a big difference between the two. The role of a police sketch artist is much different from that of a street cop or detective. Regardless of how you feel about an eyewitness or their truthfulness, you must always strive to create a positive atmosphere.

As such, a police sketch artist must constantly be aware of body language, cultural dynamics and the eyewitness's ability to express themselves. Making a mistake with any combination of the above can ruin the delicate trust you've worked to develop.

To establish this link, you must connect with the eyewitness quickly and establish a relationship. That's why it's very important to first introduce yourself and spend some time talking to them. The police sketch artist needs to set the tone at the outset and personalize the interview.

I always take the time to explain what will take place as well as what they can expect and what not to expect. Many witnesses come to an interview expecting to produce a portrait-quality likeness of the suspect. Managing their expectations always helps because I believe that if the eyewitness doesn't know what to expect, they can quickly become bored or frustrated when progress is slow.

Sometimes this process becomes slowed because it takes longer to connect with some eyewitnesses. But once a link is established, it's time to begin the interview while you guide them and set the pace.

Most police sketch artists, myself included, use some form of the cognitive interview. This method of investigative interviewing was developed in the 1980s by two psychology professors, Dr. Ronald Fisher and Dr. Edward Geiselman, as a means of enhancing eyewitness memory of crimes. Studies have shown this interview style elicits more accurate information compared with the standard form of police interview and has been found to be an effective way of interviewing people while developing suspect sketches.

A cognitive interview is successful because it's driven by the eyewitness's narrative. There are no leading questions. The interviewer can and should ask questions for clarification, but otherwise the victim/witness is allowed to relate their experience while the interviewer simply listens.

An example of this would be, "Tell me what you can

about the person's face," versus, "Was his face round?" "Were his eyes blue?" As they describe the face, they may tell you about the eye color as well as other facial features. Missed facts can be revisited and further clarified later in the interview by asking questions that are more specific.

During an interview, I've found that words of encouragement and positive body language also help reassure the witnesses and victims that they're helping.

To encourage their participation and to reinforce their recall memory, I show them a select number of photographs. Many police sketch artists have successfully used this technique , which was introduced by forensic artists at the Federal Bureau of Investigation in the late 1950s.

These images are called reference photographs. Used to aid a person's recognition skills, these photographs are often used to enhance and reinforce a person's recall in situations such as when they tell us, "I can't tell you what it looked like, but I can show you."

When used in a carefully controlled fashion, memory experts polled found this to be an effective way to produce police sketches. Police sketch artists all over the world have been using this method for years, and most I know do it responsibly and are cautious about bombarding the eyewitness with needless images. Carefully showing the eyewitness select photographic references can limit the chance of confusing them or creating a false image of someone who doesn't exist.

Besides being practical, showing them photos is a good way of drawing the eyewitnesses into the interview and engaging them in a valuable exchange of information.

My goal has always been to empower victims and eyewitnesses. I want them to feel they have a role in solving their own cases. Using reference photos helps draw their interest in the development of the sketch. Many victims and witnesses comment on how helpful this resource becomes. They grow more comfortable during the interview, and you can see them scooting their chairs closer and leaning towards you.

They may start out saying they can't recall what a suspect looks like, but before they realize it, a couple of hours have passed and they've come up with a helpful likeness of their assailant. Many victims later describe experiencing a cathartic feeling as a result of working with a police sketch artist.

I've had victims come to my office and tell me they've struggled for days, or sometimes weeks, to hold on to their memory of an assailant. Working with a police sketch artist allows them to turn the tables on the suspect and confront them again, even if it's only on paper.

With the victim's memory captured on paper, they can walk away with a positive feeling about their contribution and begin the healing process, while I sharpen my pencil and move on to the next case.

Chapter 5
Pimp-Style Hustlers

The youthful offender is probably the most dangerous class of criminal roaming the streets today. Lacking the inhibitions most adults possess, they are easily influenced and as a generation are far more desensitized to violence. With no sense of consequence for their actions and possessing keen, predatory instincts, these offenders have been conditioned by a system that's reluctant to hold them accountable for their misdeeds. They became even more dangerous when they join criminal street gangs.

Neighborhood and ethnic gangs have existed for decades, but law enforcement witnessed a steep growth in their membership and violent activities in the 1990s.

Police departments responded by forming anti-gang units to help stem the growth of gangs and curb their violence.

During this period, I was assigned to the Orange Police Department's street gang enforcement unit. My job was to focus on known gang members by patrolling the areas they lived in. As a gang officer, I worked alongside detectives, parole and probation officers to identify and arrest gang members involved in violent crime.

Sometimes, I was called away to provide sketches for other detectives. Being a police sketch artist was then a part-time, ancillary duty that required me to switch hats with little notice. One minute I was a hardened street cop, the next a sympathetic listener.

But even in an interview setting, the streets were never far away as many of the suspects I had to sketch were involved in some sort of gang activity. This kind of crossover allowed me to affect crime from two different directions. Sometimes my efforts weren't good enough. Despite our efforts to curb gang influence, they continued to grow.

Such was the case of a gang that formed in 1993 in Moreno Valley, California, called the Pimp-Style Hustlers. This gang differed from most in that it didn't form along racial lines or neighborhood boundaries. The group of about twelve youths was multi-ethnic, both males and females, ranging in age from thirteen to eighteen. And they were better organized than most, holding regular meetings at a residence in a quiet, middle-class neighborhood, at a home belonging to the mother of one of the young women.

The mother worked as a live-in housekeeper five days a week at a residence outside the city. This left her seventeen-year-old daughter home alone, unsupervised, during the week.

Before long, she was playing host to the gang at her home. They would hold regular meetings and began planning the wave of violent crime they were preparing to unleash upon the community. From the beginning, their presence had a negative impact as they turned what was once a quiet neighborhood into one that was terrorized by vandalism and the sounds of nightly gunfire.

They were led by Jack Emmit Williams, a charismatic eighteen-year-old who started the gang and began orchestrating its criminal activities. Respected by adults in his neighborhood as well as teachers at his high school, Williams' presence at a gathering would lead some gang members' parents to extend their curfew time. They trusted him, and he was always careful enough to send their children home on time. Actually, what they didn't realize was that his seeming responsibility was a cunning way to avoid arousing parental suspicion and to prevent members from being kept away from the gang.

Those who knew Williams described him as a perfect gentleman, while others described him as being intelligent and streetwise. But Williams had a darker side that he cleverly concealed as he continued to fool everyone with his "good guy" charade.

He regularly mentored others in the gang and gave lessons on how to commit crimes. He would wave his gun around often to emphasize his points and instructed them to kill anyone who did not cooperate and leave no witnesses.

Williams was an entrepreneur of sorts and envisioned his gang as different from the rest. He organized it to resemble a corporation. He structured it with both management and line levels of operation. To work your way up you had to earn "stripes," which were given for robbing or shooting someone.

Their plan was to begin with carjackings and robberies. The young members of the Pimp-Style Hustlers were excited about the prospect of earning thousands of dollars and many of them opened fresh bank accounts in anticipation of the money that would soon be flowing in.

To hide the source of the money, they decided it would be "washed" first. This money laundering process would funnel the cash through a landscaping business Williams allegedly owned with his father.

When it did return, the money would then be invested in the stock market and the profits reaped would be reinvested by purchasing more weapons to be used in more lucrative targets garnishing bigger financial rewards. Their ultimate goal was to rob an Amtrak train.

After several meetings, they set out on their first attempt at committing a crime. They began by trying to kidnap a woman. Failing at that, they tried again the following night and were able to pull off a successful carjacking. Flush from that success, they tried again. Like the previous night, they botched another attempt at a carjacking.

Not a good start, it seemed, for this ambitious group of misfits.

While researching material for this book, I spent considerable time reviewing the crime reports. Based on my experience, I wasn't sure how they planned to get money by carjacking vehicles. Within the case files there was no mention anywhere about a connection that would buy the cars or strip their parts for cash.

In addition, the only car they successfully stole, they abandoned. I had to agree with a detective working the case who described their overall operation as "unsophisticated and sloppy."

Undeterred by the gang's lack of success with carjackings, Williams went out a couple of nights later with Alonso Dearaujo Jr., age eighteen, and together they robbed a small convenience store.

With only one gun and a couple of small targets, the group was off to a slow start. Though low on cash, they were high on the smell of fear. Their crime spree put the city on edge and captured the attention of Moreno Valley's City Council, which began talking about contracting for more police and beefing up patrols.

Meanwhile, the Hustlers planned another attack.

Their next victim was Yvonne Los, a thirty-two-year-old single parent of two children, ages five and eleven. The thirteen-year veteran Air Force sergeant was stationed at March Air Force Base in Moreno Valley. She was engaged to be married, and her fiancé was also in the Air Force and worked on base with her. Both were devoutly religious and active in their local Catholic church. She also enjoyed working out and going to the gym.

On May 19, 1993, Los climbed into her gray 1987 Mercury Sable to drive to the local Family Fitness Center for her workout. Her fiancé waved to the smiling woman as she drove off into the twilight. He had no idea what tragedy lay ahead as he said goodbye to Los for what would be the last time. By now, the Pimp-Style Hustlers were out looking for another score.

On that night, it was Dearaujo Jr. and thirteen-year-old Chris Lyons who took the gang's .380 caliber Beretta handgun and went searching for a victim. In the last seven days, the gang had committed four felony crimes with little success. Among the most ardent members of the group, some described Dearaujo Jr. as the perfect street soldier for Williams to recruit. Young and impressionable, he was considered "mentally slow" and didn't do well in school while striving to fit in.

After completing her workout, Los returned to her car. She had slipped inside and started the engine when suddenly she was confronted by Dearaujo Jr. standing at her window while Lyons acted as a lookout on the passenger side. Dearaujo Jr., armed with the semi-automatic handgun, demanded that Los get out of the car.

Nearby, an employee of the Family Fitness Center had just left a tanning salon appointment and was walking to her car when she noticed the male suspects. She watched nervously and increased her pace as their presence made her uneasy and she sensed a crime was about to occur.

Parked near Los, she had a clear view of both suspects as they stood on each side of Los' car. She could hear the man on the driver's side, Dearaujo Jr., saying, "Get out of the car.

Just get out of the car."

The witness, getting into her car, made eye contact with Lyons as he stood watch on the passenger side of Los' vehicle. As she quickly started the car, she heard a gunshot, looked up and saw Lyons running away across the parking lot with Dearaujo Jr. close behind. She watched as they ran toward a nearby field and disappeared into the night.

The horn on Los' vehicle began to sound almost immediately after Los was shot, and her vehicle suddenly lurched backward. Accelerating in reverse, it struck a parked car before stopping.

When the witness saw that both suspects were gone, she pulled out of her space and drove past the other car. She saw the driver's side window was shattered and Los was slumped forward over the steering wheel, apparently wounded. Frightened by what she just had witnessed, she drove to a nearby convenience store and called the Riverside County Sheriff's Department.

Deputies responded quickly to the scene and found several panicked onlookers surrounding Los' vehicle. They shouted to the deputy that Los had been shot. One bystander was applying direct pressure to her wound in an unsuccessful effort to save her life. Unfortunately, Los was already dead. Unable to find her pulse, a member of the responding ambulance/paramedic crew officially pronounced her dead.

The witness who had driven away returned to the scene moments later and became an important part of the investigation. She was able to give deputies, and later detectives, a valuable eyewitness account of what occurred. She immediately provided deputies with a detailed description of the assailants. She included their approximate ages, height and weight, with a complete clothing description. From this, deputies were able to build a suspect profile.

Searching the crime scene, deputies found a single bullet

hole in the still rolled-up driver's side window of Los' car, through which Los had been shot in the neck. On the ground near the driver's side of the car was a spent cartridge from a .380 caliber semiautomatic pistol. Otherwise, there was little evidence left at the scene that could point police toward the killers.

The following day a forensic pathologist performed an autopsy on Los. The cause of death was a single gunshot wound to the left side of her neck. The bullet entered her neck just below her left ear, tore into her carotid artery and continued traveling through her larynx before coming to rest in the right side of her neck.

As the community reacted with fear and outrage at the callous nature of the crime, the Riverside County Sheriff's Department threw all its resources into the case. Within hours there were over twenty detectives assigned to track down the cold-blooded killers.

At the time of the killing, no one had tied the gang's many crimes together. By all appearances they had been random acts, although occurring in the same area. The racial diversity of the gang members created a variety of suspect descriptions that made it difficult to tell the perpetrators were part of the same group.

For that reason, preserving and recording eyewitness evidence became critical in this case. The witness met with a crime scene technician soon afterward to assemble a composite image of the suspect she saw standing on the passenger side of Los' car.

Detectives were unhappy with the results of their first composite sketch. The next day, detectives contacted me to see if I could re-interview their eyewitness to try to create a more detailed sketch.

Normally, I won't enter an investigation to re-do a composite image unless there's a new witness or a computerized or other mechanical system yields an image that the witness is just not happy with.

However, I was moved by the circumstances surrounding this particular murder, so I eagerly agreed to assist them. How could I say no? The crime left two small children without a mother and a community on edge.

I met the witness at the Moreno Valley Police Department, and we were led to an interview room. She appeared calm and poised, which I thought was quite remarkable considering what she'd witnessed. But she had been raised in a law enforcement family and often heard stories of violence that her father brought home from work. Over the next couple of hours, we talked and shared experiences. Working together, we constructed an image. Her detailed description was consistent with the one she gave at the crime scene: a youthful-looking, male, Hispanic teen, wearing a dark baseball cap and flannel shirt. When our session concluded and she was satisfied with the sketch, I turned it over to detectives.

The media blitz that followed provided detectives with the tip they were looking for – a suspect's name.

During a follow-up interview, the tipster told detectives that on the night of the killing, she had heard the sound of police sirens nearby. About five minutes later, a person she knew as Dearaujo Jr., accompanied by a male teen she didn't know, came to her door asking to be let inside. Dearaujo Jr. seemed agitated and said, "I just killed someone. I shot a girl at Family Fitness."

When the detectives pressed her for the other suspect's identity, she replied, "You got the picture (police sketch) of him on television. His name is Chris. I don't know his last name, and I don't know where he lives either." She did estimate that he was twelve or thirteen years old, something that shocked the detectives.

Those who knew "Chris" later told police that he later kept repeating in apparent disbelief, "I can't believe we killed someone." It was almost as if his false sense of bravado finally caught up with him and he realized the horror of what had occurred. Or maybe he was just that ruthless.

Luckily for detectives, teens love to talk and cannot keep a secret. It wasn't long before detectives identified and arrested all twelve of the Pimp-Style Hustlers gang members who were believed to be involved in the eight-day "reign of terror."

Murder charges were later filed against the gang's leader, Williams, and Dearaujo Jr. and Lyons were also charged with killing Los.

Now that they were in custody, all of them admitted their involvement in the various crimes to police as they detailed the group's activities. Most of them agreed that Williams was the group's leader and responsible for planning many of the crimes. He had given group members instructions on how to handle the gun, including his most chilling instruction. He told members of the group to "cap" or shoot anyone who did not cooperate or give up their car.

Through further interviews, detectives learned that Williams was present on the night of Los' killing and selected her car because he needed one to drive to Anaheim later that night. He gave the gun to Dearaujo Jr. and Lyons and then sat at a distance, watching the crime unfold from another car in the darkened parking lot.

After the shooting, Williams tried to convince other members of the group that the police sketch did not look like either Dearaujo Jr. or Lyons. However, police reports cited the usefulness of the sketch, with a detective later writing, referring to Lyons, that "another person resembling the composite was arrested and released. A suspect was later identified and arrested for murder. He also resembles the sketch."

During later interviews with Dearaujo Jr. and Lyons, they readily admitted their involvement in the murder and botched carjacking attempt. Dearaujo Jr. explained that he was following Williams' instructions when he shot Los because she could have identified him.

Police soon fanned out and began visiting a variety of homes in their search for evidence. Armed with several search warrants, and in some cases parental consent, they located and seized several pieces of evidence, but not the gun used to murder Los.

Five days after the shooting, authorities' hard work and efforts paid off when two juvenile informants told the police where to find the murder weapon. The two brothers knew all of the people associated with the Pimp-Style Hustlers and even had been recruited to join them.

Their interview helped police put the week's crimes together while painting a frightening image of Lyons, the group's youngest member.

They told detectives that on May 21, 1993, they had been hanging out at Lyons' home. Two nights had passed since Los' murder, yet Lyons seemed relaxed as he tried to recruit the brothers into the gang to participate in carjackings.

Chatting excitedly, Lyons told them they could soon be "rolling in thousands of dollars in just a few weeks." Thinking he was joking and not really serious, they laughed and played along, pretended to agree, telling Lyons, "Yeah, carjackings."

Lyons told them he was serious and it wasn't funny. His mood darkened he gave them the ominous warning, "This better not get out or you could get shot."

When they realized he was serious, they begged off and said they couldn't do it. Lyons told them that it was too late, they had to do it because now they knew all the details. They again insisted that they didn't want to participate.

Later that evening all three went to a nearby house and met up with Williams and another young man. Williams told Lyons to go to the house of a female associate, get the gun and take it to another gang member's home nearby.

The young woman took the gun from its hiding place in the attic. Shuttling the weapon to another home, it was quickly becoming a high stakes game of "Keep Away" as they tried to remain one step ahead of police. They knew the gun was the linchpin of the case and detectives would need it for a successful prosecution if they were caught.

At the second house, they passed the gun through the front window. The two brothers remembered Lyons talking with the man who took the gun.

Later, the brothers led detectives back to that house.

Detectives knocked on the door and spoke to the young man who answered. After a brief conversation, he admitted having the gun. He allowed them inside and led detectives to his bedroom, where they found a weapon behind a desk, below the front window. The .380 caliber Beretta semiautomatic pistol had been disassembled.

The young man admitted to detectives that he'd taken the gun apart in an attempt to conceal the fact that he had handled it. By disassembling it, he hoped to remove his fingerprints.

As it turned out, detectives had already questioned him the night after Lyons gave him the gun. He said he didn't mention it at the time because he didn't want to go to jail. But after police seized the gun and seven unexpended rounds, he was arrested anyway. He was later booked for his involvement in various crimes committed by the gang.

The biggest tragedy in this case was how Los' promising young life was cut short without a second thought. Meanwhile, her young children were sent overseas to be with their father, who was stationed in Germany. And, despite pleading guilty to their crimes, many members of the Pimp-Style Hustlers are back out on the street today.

Hopefully they've become productive members of society. Even though many of them are young adults, I hope their parents will try to reclaim the time they lost and become a positive force in their lives.

Williams and Dearaujo Jr. are serving life sentences in an adult state prison, but Lyons was sent to serve his time in the California State Youth Authority, a facility referred to in California law enforcement circles as "kiddy prison." Although the goal of the system is rehabilitation, I don't have much faith that there is a whole lot of rehabilitation going on. In my opinion, such facilities are factories that serve to breed more-sophisticated criminals.

Lyons was ordered to remain there until he was at least twenty-five years old. During his sentencing, the judge lashed out at him in frustration, calling Lyons a "cold and callous" individual.

When he's released, what will he have learned? I don't know, maybe nothing.

All parents should consider that something had gone wrong in these youths' families. Is there a catalyst to be found somewhere? What was it that caused many of them to turn to a life filled with violence? We will probably never know.

One thing we do know is that the community stepped up to protect itself.

Sgt. Tom Arnold told the Riverside Press Enterprise newspaper the break in the case came "when a tipster recognized one of the murder suspects in a composite drawing published in a newspaper." He thanked the media and told them they had been a tremendous asset in the investigation.

The successful conclusion of the case was the direct

result of strong community support. I am always in awe of the positive results that occur when good citizens step forward to partner with law enforcement. Much can be accomplished through strong community partnerships. When people feel empowered to stand up to these cowardly acts, they ensure other good people will not die in vain.

And to me, that's the ultimate act of citizenship.

MICHAEL W. STREED

Chapter 6
Brothers to the Bone

It's often been said that dead men tell no tales.

And, while that may have been true in a time when swashbuckling pirates ruled the high seas, modern day forensic science techniques have developed to the point where, now, the dead are talking all the time.

Obviously, the dead cannot literally speak for themselves. Sometimes they need someone to speak for them, especially when their identity becomes a mystery. For those trying to put a name to unidentified human remains, finding family and friends is a most important task.

In cases of murder, finding out the identity of the remains also aids in finding the killer.

Luckily for those unnamed victims, techniques have been developed over the last several years allowing us to restore the facial appearance to bones in order to learn a victim's identity. These methods have restored many identities to those officially referred to as "John or Jane Doe," giving them back in death the only thing they had left – their name in life.

Throughout this book, there's been much discussion about suspect sketches and the role they've played in catching crooks. However, there's also another element to what we do as police sketch artists, and that occurs when we are called upon to assist with the identification of unidentified bodies. This involves the painstaking task of reconstructing a face using a skull as the foundation.

Throughout the world today, many such facial approximation techniques are used. In the United States, two popular, widely used techniques have proved successful over the years.

The first technique involves the sculpting of a three-dimensional clay recreation of the head. Placing strips of clay over the surface of the skull, the artist can simulate both muscle and surface tissue. Depth markers placed at various locations on the skull simulate the thickness to be expected at those predetermined sites.

Each skull is unique, and those subtle differences help the artist prepare a "lifelike" replica of the head. If the artist has strong sculpting skills and uses accessories such as wigs and prosthetic eyes, the result can look frighteningly real.

The second technique is a method in which the information is presented in a two-dimensional format, with the artist basing a carefully rendered portrait on the skull and any other available information.

I've tried both methods during actual cases with varied results. My first facial approximation was an attempt to identify a murder victim. The woman's mostly decomposed body was found off an unforgiving stretch of desert highway near Blythe.

Coroner's technicians gave me her "cleaned" skull, and I anxiously began the process.

Over the course of several days, I lay down strips of clay, kneading and smoothing it until the artistic creation began to take on a human form.

Using prosthetic eyes for a more realistic look, I topped the head off with a synthetic wig. To finish off "her" appearance, I used makeup to touch up her lips with some color and shrouded her shoulders with a shirt collar. When I finished, she projected a very realistic looking appearance. She was later trotted out for display to the media with the hope someone might recognize her and call in with a tip, giving her a name.

When she wasn't on display, she sat atop a file cabinet, her face to the corner like a misbehaved child. The supervising deputy coroner explained to me that it was placed that way because "her" steady gaze would unnerve even the most seasoned deputy coroner. They weren't used to their dead being brought back to life.

Despite investigators' best efforts, though, she remains unidentified.

It wouldn't be long before I had the opportunity to assist with another identification of remains. This time I used the two-dimensional technique.

During the spring of 1993, Southern California was flooded by a series of torrential rainstorms. The outlying desert areas of Riverside County were hit particularly hard. Much property was destroyed as low-lying areas became raging rivers. When it was over, people began leaving their homes to survey the damage.

One day, two young boys playing in a wash area near Winchester made a grisly discovery. As they neared a dirt embankment, they saw skeletal remains exposed by the rainstorm.

They ran home and called the Riverside County Sheriff's Department, which sent deputies to check. After confirming the discovery, they immediately protected the area as if it were a crime scene. Because many American Indian tribes originate in the area, it was initially thought to be an ancient Indian burial site.

But to know for sure, authorities would need to excavate

the body and examine it to determine its origin.

Deputies notified the Coroner's Office, whose job it would be to identify the remains. Coroner's deputies inspected the site and determined they would need the help of a forensic anthropologist.

They called upon Dr. Judy Suchey, a highly respected anthropology professor at California State University at Fullerton. As a board certified forensic anthropologist, she was considered "tops" in her field.

After inspecting the scene and consulting with authorities, she determined that in order to best preserve evidence, she would need to bring a forensic anthropology recovery team, which was comprised of university students trained in recovery methods. For this particular burial site, Suchey decided an "archeological excavation" would be preferable to the standard "shovel out" method. Although more costly and time-consuming, she felt it was the best way to locate and preserve valuable evidence.

When the full bodies were revealed, authorities quickly realized it was not a sacred Indian burial ground at all. The burial site was a murder scene.

Two clothed skeletons lay head to feet on top of each other. The clothing bore insignias leading investigators to believe the two were involved with outlaw motorcycle gangs.

Further examination of the gravesite led investigators to believe it had been trenched with a backhoe for the specific purpose of permanently hiding the bodies. If not for the rains, the killer or killers might have been successful. Evidence at the scene was scant and consisted only of the clothing, a distinctive piece of jewelry and a bullet rattling around in one of the skulls.

After the remains were photographed and measured, they were taken to the coroner's facility for an autopsy by pathologists and evaluation by the forensic anthropologist.

It was later determined that the victims, both men, had been shot in the head. One had an execution-style entrance wound at the lower left base of his skull. The bullet traveled through his head and lodged in his right cheekbone. The bullet was recovered and appeared to have come from either a .38 caliber or .357 handgun. The other skull bore "multiple defects," which the doctor felt may have indicated a gunshot wound, but the only bullet found was in the other skull.

After the autopsy, it was time for the forensic anthropologist to get to work.

Upon her initial examination, Suchey could see the skulls were in poor condition. She estimated the remains had been buried for anywhere from seven to seventeen years. The remaining bones themselves were quite fragile and had to be examined carefully.

Bones can tell forensic anthropologists much about a person's sex, gender, age, height, weight and personal lifestyle, including probable professions, hobbies and even disabilities. Suchey's examination determined that both were white males, similar in age and height. Her findings provided detectives and coroner's officials the first clues to their identities.

Mike Oare, a Riverside County Sheriff's Department coroner's investigator, was tasked with identifying the victims, whose deaths were classified by pathologists as criminal homicides.

Oare's first step was to send the jawbone and upper teeth to a forensic odontologist, who examined and X-rayed them. He created dental charts, which were later sent to the California Justice Department's Missing and Unidentified Persons Unit. Unfortunately, there was not a match to anyone who had been reported missing in California.

That meant that either they were not from the state or that no one had reported them missing.

How could no one have reported them missing? They had been buried for so long, surely someone had to have missed them and cared enough to make a report to the police.

What seemed to be a simple task became a two-year odyssey in the quest to identify the two bodies. Stories in the press and hundreds of hours spent poring over law enforcement teletypes failed to generate the leads necessary to identify them.

In a last-ditch effort to identify the bodies, Oare called me and asked to meet to discuss the case.

I took an immediate liking to Oare. He was a sincere and hardworking investigator. He was determined to solve this case and find out what had happened to the two so he could return the bodies to their families.

As a courtesy, he provided me with a stack of police and coroner's reports, complete with photographs of the crime scene and autopsies.

Finally, it was time to see the skulls. At the time, the Coroner's Office was headquartered in an old mortuary in downtown Riverside. Oare led me to a dank, dimly lit attic area where weathered wood shelves housed long forgotten evidence and many unidentified skulls. The room was cold, dusty and smelled like death -- a perfect setting for a horror movie.

After our meeting was over, I boxed up the skulls, gathered up the reports and photos, and took them home, where I had a dedicated studio and room to work.

Once there, I laid the pieces out and carefully began a series of steps that I hoped would identify them.

First, I reassembled the skulls.

In a review of the anthropology and pathology reports, I found the victims' sex and probable build.

For the probable tissue depths of their faces, I referred to a series of charts developed by forensic anthropologists.

Clothing that shrouded the skeletal remains helped me determine that their builds were normal or average.

Age determination would later help me place any facial lines or wrinkles in their appropriate location when rendering the final illustration.

After sketching for several days, I was able to complete renderings of both faces based upon information provided by the forensic clues. Yet, there was still something missing.

The hair. What about their hair? None remained at the scene. It would be up to me to decide what length and style to illustrate. Referring back to the forensic anthropologist's report estimating how long they had been buried, I went with the high end of seventeen years. Subtracting the time from when the bones were found placed the date of the murders in the mid-1970s.

I pulled my dusty 1976 high school annual from its storage box in my garage. The photos reminded me of the popular male hairstyle of the day -- straight, parted in the middle and hanging to the shoulders. I also knew that to be a popular hairstyle with many biker-types I'd encountered over the course of my police career.

I was able finally to finish the drawings of two young men who shared similar facial characteristics and hairstyles. I scheduled a meeting with Oare so I could return the drawings and photographs.

When I delivered them, he carefully scrutinized them and showed them off to a couple of other investigators. After several quiet moments, he opined that they "looked an awful lot alike."

I caught a hint of skepticism in his voice, and I flippantly replied, "Who knows, maybe they're brothers" as I headed out the door.

*Author's facial reconstruction sketch is on the left,
Charles Taylor's photo is on the right.*

A press release was created, and the media carried the story of the bones' discovery. A description of the remains was also included with the sketches I supplied. Clothing details, including the Harley Davidson T-shirt, biker boots and a marijuana leaf "pinky-style" ring, would provide further clues to their identities.

After two years, Oare's efforts paid off. A recently retired woman had moved to Riverside County and read the story. The sketches and story stirred a vague memory that was triggered by the mention of the distinctive ring. Could the bodies be Charlie and Allan Taylor, two acquaintances from years past? She showed the sketches to her son-in-law to confirm her suspicions and then called the Coroner's Office.

At the same time in Orange County, a retired district attorney's investigator recalled a murder case he assisted with several years before involving a suspect tried and convicted for the murders of Charles and Allan Taylor, two brothers abducted at gunpoint in Huntington Beach in 1978. He also called Oare with his suspicions.

Meanwhile, I had gone about my business, sketching crooks and catching crooks. I was alerted to the developments in the case one day by a newspaper reporter who called me at home to ask for comment about the identification of the Taylor brothers.

Brothers? I thought back to the offhand remark I'd made to Oare as I was leaving his office that day several months back, and now it all made sense.

I later learned the connection to the abduction and murder case wasn't made initially due to an oversight. The brothers' dental records remained in a file and had not been forwarded to the State Department of Justice after their kidnapping in 1978. Investigators following up on the telephone tips finally confirmed their identities.

From police reports files at the time of the kidnapping and later newspaper articles, I learned that Charles and Allan Taylor had been taken at gunpoint one night in front of several witnesses.

One of those present that night was Nancy Arroyo, Charles Taylor's girlfriend and mother of their infant son, Charles Jr. She had met Charles after his older brother Ryan Taylor moved in next door when she was a sixteen-year-old high school student.

Charles, whom she referred to as Charlie, soon began hanging out at the house. She became attracted to him and fell in love with his free-spirited thinking. Charlie loved being outdoors and she said nothing could hold him down. Charlie had a "huge" heart, she said, and would give anyone anything they needed if it was his to give. Other than some minor scrapes with the law, their life was good together.

Ignoring those who thought he was trouble and urged her

to leave him, she stayed, and they had two children together. Their daughter, Gina, died tragically as an infant, and their son, Charles Jr., grew up in the likeness of his father and inherited his mechanical skills and love for motorcycles.

Charlie was devoted to Ryan, his older half brother, and soon began to accompany him and another unidentified person on home invasion robberies. Under the cover of darkness, the three would go to the homes of other motorcycle enthusiasts, surprise them, tie them up and take their motorcycles.

Arroyo said they would work late into the night taking the motorcycles apart, repainting them and switching the vehicle identification numbers before selling the motorcycles, sometimes just selling the parts.

On one occasion, they went to the home of Thomas Pugh, an alleged member of the Hangmen Motorcycle Club, a local outlaw biker gang. They tied up Pugh and a couple of women. During the robbery, Ryan allegedly shot Pugh, but the wound was not fatal. They took some cash and Pugh's motorcycle before leaving. The women were able to free themselves and see a pickup truck as it left the area, and they knew who the owner was.

The Hangmen began to look for Ryan immediately. They searched Orange County, allegedly beating several people in their efforts to find him.

On the evening of March 9, 1978, Arroyo told police she got a phone call from a woman who told her, "Two guys are hot on Charlie's trail. The two of you better get out of the house because if you don't the baby will be without a father." She told Arroyo that she had tried unsuccessfully to convince the men that Charlie hadn't stolen the bike, then hung up the phone.

About an hour later, Arroyo, Charlie, his brother Allan and a male acquaintance were in the alleyway to the rear of their apartments. Arroyo secured Charles Jr. inside the vehicle and began arguing with Charlie about his involvement in the "rip-offs." Charlie was standing in the open carport bordering a darkened field, and Arroyo was sitting inside the car with the baby. Out of the darkness, two men approached them. One of them, armed with a small revolver with a two-inch barrel, fired a shot at the same time he announced, "Hold it, we're the police."

A neighbor who had been talking to the brothers was forced to the pavement and told to keep his head down.

Arroyo was jerked out of the car by the second suspect. Grabbing a length of her hair, he threw her to the pavement and told her, "Don't move or I'll blow your head off."

The two approached Charlie and Allan from behind and asked their names. When the brothers answered, they were handcuffed and led away toward the field, disappearing into the darkness and were never seen again.

Arroyo jumped up and began to run for a phone to call the police, but the second suspect peeked around the corner of the fence and said, "If you don't get your face down, I'll shoot it!"

She got back down and waited about thirty more seconds before jumping up again and running toward the front of the apartments to see if she could catch a glimpse of any vehicles leaving the area. She saw what she described as a 1970s white or yellow van with no side windows and a horizontal stripe leaving the area in an easterly direction.

A police sergeant responding to the call passed by a similar looking vehicle leaving the area which he described as a light-colored, possibly green van with out-of-state license plates with a yellow background. It's not known why he didn't detain the vehicle, but he likely didn't realize the van contained the suspects until it was too late.

Police arrived and found a crime scene that didn't yield many clues. Responding officers were unable to find any spent shell casings to support the witnesses' statement that the weapon was a revolver. There were also no footprints found because it had been raining.

During the initial stages of the investigation, detectives used hypnosis on Arroyo to assist her memory for facts that might not have been revealed during the primary interview.

Detectives also located the female caller. She said that Pugh and an associate, Steven Earle, had come to her workplace and asked if she would help locate Ryan. She said they pressured her into helping to set Ryan up because they thought he was responsible for shooting Pugh. She took them to five or six places, but they were unable to locate him.

Pugh and Earle were detained by police and interviewed about the kidnapping. Both denied participating in or having any knowledge of what happened. Earle said little, while Pugh told them he had been trying to get the woman to help him find Ryan so he could provide the police with information about the shooting.

Police found a vehicle at Earle's home that was similar to the one described by Arroyo and the police sergeant. The vehicle, a green Dodge van with Arizona license plates, was impounded for examination while an attempt was made to collect any corroborating evidence. Authorities also seized a semi-automatic handgun from inside his home.

Police arrested Earle and Pugh for conspiracy to commit kidnapping. At the time of their arrest, a handcuff key was found on Earle's key ring during the booking process.

Rumors swirled about the brothers' fate. One story that was consistent said the brothers were dead. Pugh was said to have been seeking revenge for the shooting and robbery at his home and killed the brothers in retaliation.

Ryan took in Arroyo and Charles Jr. to live with him after the kidnapping. Arroyo said that Ryan cried often about his brothers' fate. He felt responsible for their deaths, knowing he was the one the men were looking for. Ryan was later murdered during an unrelated drug deal in Los Angeles.

After a lengthy investigation and trial, Pugh was convicted of kidnapping and murdering Charles and Allan Taylor. Though Earle was arrested soon after the brothers went missing, he was never prosecuted.

Pugh was sentenced to a term of twenty-five years to life for the killings. Four years into his sentence the California State Court of Appeals agreed to hear his case.

Pugh's lawyers appealed because prosecutors had failed to tell his lawyers that Arroyo and another female witness had been hypnotized during the original investigation. After Pugh's conviction, the California Supreme Court had ruled in a similar case that testimony gained from hypnotized witnesses was inadmissible. The court ruled they had suppressed evidence that could not be used in a retrial, and Pugh was ordered released immediately.

When the bodies were found, they didn't yield enough evidence to retry Pugh, who remains free today. The original trial judge, who was forced to dismiss the charges, later commented, "It was a shame for the case to be dismissed on anything other than its merits."

The original prosecutor expressed frustration that "the people have a right to a fair trial" and would not get their day in court if prosecutors weren't allowed to use the previous testimony that was the crux of the case.

Several years later I met with Arroyo, and she thanked me for my efforts and told me what it meant to have the closure her family needed. She told me that Charlie's parents were both deceased and all of their sons had been murdered or killed in military combat with the exception of one. At the time of the murders, that son was away in the Army. But she felt sure that he would have been with Charlie and Allan the night they were kidnapped.

Arroyo focused her time on raising Charles Jr., who refused to believe his father was dead. Up until the time his father's body was found, he lived for the day that his father would walk through the door and they could be a family again.

Sometimes it was hard for Arroyo to see their son grow into the image and lifestyle of his father. Arroyo was also hurt when authorities labeled the Taylors as "bikers." She asserted that neither one had ever been a member of an outlaw motorcycle gang. While she did acknowledge some criminal behavior, she didn't believe that Charlie or Allan deserved to be killed.

Arroyo credited my facial approximation sketches with helping bring the case to a final conclusion. While it didn't change what happened, it did bring her family closure and allowed them to properly grieve the deaths and continue to move on with their lives.

My job is not always about catching crooks. The ability to restore dignity to the dead and help others heal is an added element of what I do. But, most important, I have the opportunity to provide the dead a voice by which to speak the most important words of all – their name.

Chapter 7
Pencils or Pixels?

So, which method works best for producing police sketches, facial composite software programs or a freehand sketch produced by a trained police sketch artist?

That's one of those questions I've been asked several times over the years by curious observers.

The question always amuses me because it reminds me of a grocery store clerk asking, "Paper or plastic?" before stuffing my items into one of them.

My answer to the question is, both methods work. But, like the grocery bag analogy, it depends on what or how much you put in the particular bag or, in the case of a police composite sketch, how much information an eyewitness provides and if you are able to successfully translate it into a composite image.

I've been asked many times about my composite sketches, "So, did you do that on your computer?" Many police sketch artists would be offended by such as question. But I am actually quite flattered when someone thinks highly enough of my work to confuse it with a computer-generated image. Computer images are thought by some to be more efficient and accurate than anything produced by an artist's hand, so I'll gladly take the confusion as a compliment.

While I've labored hard over the years to develop high-quality sketches, I've always been a strong advocate of law enforcement using the best resources available to meet the demands of their investigations.

Facial composite software programs have been developed for law enforcement agencies that lack access to a qualified police sketch artist. In their effort to stem the rise of crime in their communities, police are increasing their use of the technology to catch crooks by churning out images using a computer instead of a pencil.

Many companies have developed facial composite software programs without seeking technical assistance from police sketch artists. This has caused a lack of support by artists in the forensic community. But regardless of their negative opinion, this burgeoning technology, is here to stay.

I have always supported using these programs because I know it would be impossible for me to be everywhere at once and I wouldn't even try to be. What I have done to help law enforcement is develop my own facial composite software program, SketchCop Facette. I have taken the added step of providing high-quality training and support for law enforcement clients who purchase the software. Lending my expertise and support to the development of SketchCop Facette Face Design System has made it a popular solution for those agencies without a qualified police sketch artist on staff.

I have always endorsed using the best tool for the job. In a few isolated cases, I've successfully used facial composite software programs to identify crooks.

The evolution from freehand sketching to mechanical assembly kits can be traced to 1959 when the Identi-Kit was formally introduced to law enforcement in the United States.

Hugh McDonald, a Los Angeles police detective working in the LAPD Identification Bureau, analyzed thousands of photos to create a system of facial features printed on cellophane overlays. The transparent overlays, when placed on top of one another, created a composite face of a suspect. Any adjustments or added-on features would be drawn onto the overlay with a grease pencil. The final, and sometimes crude, image could then be photocopied and distributed to officers in the field.

The system was eventually acquired and marketed by the Smith & Wesson firearms manufacturing company.

Soon after, the Identi-Kit became the standard tool for police agencies wanting to develop composite images.

Up until then, police sketches had been developed by artists like myself drawing freehand. Often police investigators would borrow artists from a local newspaper or commission an artist from the community. As such, use of police sketches was reserved for only the most heinous cases.

During the early years, there also was no standardized training for police sketch artists and no organization to provide it. Since then, there have been many training courses developed throughout the United States.

Still, with a scarcity of police artists, the computer industry stepped in to try to fill the void by developing software to duplicate what an artist could do. Despite their best efforts, the early software had limitations. Lacking the warmth and personality most sketch artists possess and use when interacting with a witness, the process of developing images with a computer felt cold and mechanical.

Two of the earliest documented successes using the mechanical systems occurred in the United States and England. In both instances, the Identi-Kit system was used.

In 1958, a notorious killer began roaming Los Angeles, preying on young women. Back then, the city was still a growing metropolis with a police department in the throes of re-organization. A professional organization with a fine reputation for solving crime, the Los Angeles Police Department began an investigation on a suspect they would come to call "The Lonely Hearts Killer."

Harvey Glatman posed as a photographer for a "true detective" magazine. He would meet his female prey by placing personal ads in the newspaper. Glatman bound and gagged his victims under the pretense that they were taking part in a photo shoot for the magazine's cover.

Glatman asked them to feign frightened poses while he photographed them. Obsessed with bondage since his youth, Glatman would tie them up with rope and then gag them, saying it was for the photos. These props, however, served to trap them and prevent their screaming when their terror became real as he raped and strangled them.

Officers were able to arrest Glatman after one of his victims overpowered him and took his gun. Fearing for her life, she shot Glatman in the leg and held him until police arrived.

His arrest confirmed the remarkable accuracy of a composite image that investigators had created of the suspect using the Identi-Kit.

Glatman was later convicted for the torture and murder of several victims and executed in California's gas chamber.

After the success of the Identi-Kit in capturing the suspect's likeness during the Lonely Hearts Killer investigation, the system became a staple for law enforcement agencies needing facial composites. Soon, the Identi-Kit's use expanded overseas to England.

After a woman was found slain in her antique store in London, on March 3, 1961, investigators used the Identi-Kit to construct a composite image of a person seen inside the shop the day before the murder.

About four days later, a beat officer detained Edwin

Bush, a twenty-one-year-old petty thief who resembled the composite. Bush was positively identified as the suspect and later admitted to the murder. He was executed in July of that year.

Before his execution, Bush conceded that the image looked like him. The constable in charge of the investigation gave full credit for closing the case to the American-made facial identification system.

Several years later, English law enforcement authorities would help pioneer their own system, called E-Fit. It was developed with the assistance of Scotland Yard and is still widely used today by police throughout England.

In the United States, the Identi-Kit continues to be used by law enforcement agencies to create facial composites. In addition, over the years, many other computer software systems have been marketed to law enforcement with varying levels of success.

Yet despite the success of the Identi-Kit, the LAPD turned to a police sketch artist to develop composite images for use in their major case investigations. Their artist, Ector Garcia, was also a police officer and so, like me, had the best of both worlds.

In 1959, Garcia had been critically wounded by a drunken gunman while he and his partner investigated a murder. Left with sight in only one eye, he overcame his handicap and distinguished himself as a police sketch artist, turning out many amazingly accurate sketches.

His personal story and some of his most important cases are detailed in his book, "Portraits of Crime."

At about the same time Garcia was helping the LAPD, another major law enforcement agency on the other side of the country was working with their own artists and soon became a leader in the field of police composites.

In Washington, D.C., the Federal Bureau of

Investigation's Graphic Arts Unit employed artists known as visual information specialists. Their use grew out of the mid-1950s and early 1960s, when the FBI was tasked with politically motivated hunts to uncover members of the Communist Party while at the same time trying to stem a significant increase in the number of armed bank robberies across the country.

The busy FBI agents needed to find an efficient method of documenting a suspect's facial appearance, so a process was researched and developed for use by the visual information specialists.

The specialists were kept busy, too. Not only were they responsible for providing services to about 52 FBI field offices, but they also provided trial exhibits for U.S. Attorney's Offices. On many occasions, the FBI artists were flown across the country to assist agents. In select cases, they were used internationally.

Because the field offices were spread from coast to coast, travel costs soon became prohibitive and budgetary constraints limited the use of the artists to only the most serious crimes.

For lesser crimes, they would have to devise a system that would allow artists to complete sketches from the confines of their offices in Washington, D.C.

To accomplish that goal, they devised a system that exploited the theories about memory function described in a previous chapter. Merging a person's recall skills with their recognition skills, the system succeeded in identifying several major criminals.

The system created during the late 1950's involved a photographic reference book called the Facial Identification Catalog. The book, still used today, displays several black-and-white mug shots of convicted federal prisoners, including gangster Al Capone.

The artists divided the faces into categories based on major facial features and then further refined those divisions by breaking those down into subcategories. Each feature was coded for easy reference and later documentation.

The FBI's system was similar to one pioneered by Alphonse Bertillon in the 19 th century. As the chief of criminal identification in Paris, he applied the anthropological technique of anthropometry, taking precise measurements of a criminal's head and body and cataloging them for later comparison if someone's identity was called into question.

In 1883, Bertillon identified his first criminal "recidivist" using the system. Bertillon wanted to further refine and develop an even more useful system that would allow a person to describe a suspect without having to be present to select their photo. The system he devised was even more precise than the one before and involved a system of measurements for the face that became known as *"portrait parle,"* or "speaking likeness."

Over time, however, variations arose in the measurements when the same person was arrested over and over again. Inconsistency in the measurements and how they changed as the face aged was the beginning of the end for that system. It fell out of use after a misidentification in a case later was solved through the use of fingerprints.

However, the idea that faces could be described and identified through careful observation of the landmark features was a breakthrough in itself. Since then, the usefulness of the method has been confirmed by psychologists who specialize in memory studies and by the field results when suspects were captured and their likenesses compared to a sketch.

The Facial Identification Catalog created by the FBI was based on Bertillon's studies with further refinements. Its design was crafted to be more useful to law enforcement personnel and the police sketch artists who would be using it. Mostly though, because of its broad audience, it had to be easily understood in order to be useful, especially in instances when an artist wasn't able to travel to the crime scene or investigating field office.

In those cases, the responsibility of interviewing the eyewitness fell to the investigating special agent, who showed the book to witnesses and let them select a variety of facial features. The agent would then record their responses on a specially designed report form.

Once the interview was completed and the form was completed, the agent would use a facsimile machine to transmit the form back to the visual information specialist, who in turn would translate the coded image into a drawing.

Once drawn, the artist would send the image back to the agent to consult the witness and record any changes they required to finalize the image. Sometimes this took several exchanges back and forth, but despite the awkwardness great results were achieved.

By the mid-1980s, the FBI artists began teaching a popular class at the FBI Academy in Quantico, Virginia. It has since evolved into a three-week course that includes the basics of developing composite images as well as facial reconstruction.

I was part of the steering committee that met at the FBI Academy in 1984 to develop the first course curriculum. The primary goal for hosting and sponsoring the course was to train local police sketch artists they could call upon if their own artists weren't available.

The course remained popular for years and often required that the FBI maintain a year's long wait list of students.

As technology continued to develop, other facial composite software programs were coming onto the market and adopted for use by law enforcement agencies. This seemed to be the future, and as much as I enjoyed drawing,

I figured the best way to help shape the technology was to get involved. My thought was to provide training for law enforcement officers on how to use facial composite software.

It didn't really matter to me if agencies used a computer-generated image. All I cared about was that they were using it properly and turning out quality images based on a sound method of interviewing eyewitnesses and the practiced use of the software's editing tools to refine the composite image into something that would satisfy the eyewitness.

The problem I had with most companies was that they created unrealistic expectations for their software. They advertised "quick, easy to develop" composites that could be turned out in minutes. They ignored a key component of developing a composite, which is the eyewitness interview -- a difficult task that can sometimes take hours.

Despite the lack of training and support these companies provided to law enforcement, I believed these computer software programs could still have value.

One such product was sold by Infotec Development Inc., an Orange County company that specialized in law enforcement and defense technology solutions. Their program, FaceKit, was at that time considered to be the best facial composite software available to law enforcement. After a series of meetings, they hired me as a consultant and law enforcement trainer.

It was an ideal situation. The company's location allowed me to meet often with software engineers and sales executives. I was also allowed to create my own training curriculum. As the product's popularity grew, I began traveling around the country as a product evangelist.

In 1994, the Ventura County Sheriff's Department, located on California's central coast, purchased a copy of FaceKit software for every sheriff's station and municipal law enforcement agency in the county. The fact that they bought so many software licenses was a testament to FaceKit's popularity among law enforcement. Upon completing the sale, I spent several weeks traveling to every station, plus local police departments, training detectives and other select personnel my method for developing computerized composite images.

During a class hosted at the Ventura County Sheriff's Thousand Oaks Station, a skeptical detective told me of a recent robbery he was investigating. He asked if I could conduct a lunchtime interview with his eyewitnesses. He wanted to see if what the agency was buying really worked.

I'm not quite sure why he cared so much, since it wasn't his money used to buy the software. Maybe he was just trying to embarrass me. I didn't really think too much about it, and I enthusiastically agreed to do it. I believed in the system and wanted to demonstrate its capabilities.

We broke class for lunch at twelve o'clock. The detective brought me two witnesses: a man and a woman. I had until one o'clock to complete the composite. A couple of the students stayed and watched as the interview began and the clock started ticking.

Normally, I wouldn't agree to such conditions. It is important to maintain the eyewitnesses' privacy, but I was told the witnesses didn't mind cooperating in the detective's little experiment. Plus, they had not been traumatized by the robbery and were actually passive witnesses. Now, if it had been a rape or murder case, there would be no way I would agree to conduct an interview in such a setting.

The crime they witnessed was an armed robbery on Aug. 24, 1994, at a supermarket in the city of Moorpark. The suspect was described as a white man, approximately thirty-five years old, 5-foot-10 in height and approximately 170 pounds. He was further described as having curly, wavy, sandy brown hair, a moustache and a "five o'clock shadow."

His skin was described as being "slightly pock-marked" with an olive complexion. He wore unremarkable clothing with a baseball cap pulled down on his forehead in an attempt to hide much of his face. During the robbery, he brandished a dark, semi-automatic pistol and afterward fled the area on foot.

It was a pretty fair description of a robber who terrorized his victims with a gun. As it turned out, a couple of the witnesses told deputies the suspect was an occasional customer in the store so they'd seen him many times before.

On the night of the robbery, the man entered the store at about 10:30 p.m. and stood waiting in a well-lit checkout line with a few grocery items. While he patiently waited, the witnesses had an opportunity to watch him for over twenty minutes. They recognized him from the previous visits and had ample opportunity to make mental notes about his appearance. Once he reached the cashier, he asked to see the manager because he wanted to make restitution on a "bad check" that he said his girlfriend had written. He was directed to the customer service area, where he waited for the manager.

He talked to the manager, who asked the suspect to wait downstairs while he searched the bad check file. Ignoring him, the suspect followed the manager upstairs to his office and waited outside the door while the manager was inside.

When the manager walked out the door, he was surprised by the suspect who confronted him as he held the gun in one hand and his bag of groceries tucked under his other arm.

The suspect seemed confused and upset because he didn't get into the room where the money drops were made. For all his yelling and gun waving, the robbery only netted him about $245. The man calmly walked downstairs and was followed outside by a store employee who then chased him from the area. The suspect successfully escaped and continued his crime spree, later being identified in the robberies of a couple of banks in the city of Thousand Oaks.

Back in the safety of the classroom, we worked hard to complete the composite as both witnesses filled in gaps in each other's description.

With both, I exhausted their recall skills, which I would enhance later in the interview by showing them facial feature reference photos to draw on their recognition skills. Always careful to limit the number of photos shown, I didn't want to confuse them or create an image in their mind that didn't exist.

As we neared one o'clock, I used the software's paintbrush feature to add the final touches. We were finishing the image in time to share it with the students who were filing back inside the classroom at one o'clock.

The final result was given to the detective, and a "wanted" bulletin was generated. Several months later, Michael Todd Lopez, a former Moorpark resident, was arrested by the FBI on federal bank robbery charges.

When the lieutenant in charge of the investigation received the information and mug photo of Lopez, he noticed that it closely matched the composite I had produced with the witnesses from the supermarket robbery.

Author's computerized sketch is in the center,
Lopez's photo is on the left and right.

Lineups were conducted, and Lopez was officially identified. Deputies weren't allowed to interview him because the federal agents didn't want anything to ruin their chances of a successful prosecution.

It wouldn't matter anyway, because Lopez didn't admit to the grocery store robbery and even enlisted friends to create a false alibi for him.

Despite minimal evidence, a Ventura County deputy district attorney filed robbery charges and proceeded to trial.

Because facial identification is not an exact science like fingerprints or DNA identification, there was apprehension over how my testimony would be received. I spent time explaining the process to the county attorney, who was a quick study and understood the process perfectly.

When we finally went to trial, the defense brought in an expert witness who was a forensic psychologist. He testified that the identification of Lopez was flawed because of a psychological theory he called "weapon focus."

He went on to describe it as a phenomenon in which witnesses would have been so traumatized by the gun in Lopez's hand that they focused on it alone and didn't observe his face long enough or with enough concentration. As a result, he said, they could not correctly describe him to me well enough to develop a composite image.

What the expert forgot was that the witnesses all had the opportunity to observe him for a long period of time that day and on prior occasions with no trauma, which virtually destroyed his theory. When that didn't work, the defense attacked my comparative lack of education: Their expert had a doctorate degree while I did not, and he had conducted numerous experiments at respected educational institutions while I had not.

I wasn't bothered by their efforts to discredit me because I had achieved success many times during previous cases. I was able to back my claims with a portfolio of those results, which were shown to the jury.

I was able to articulate and explain to the jury my consistent method for developing facial images. My results were field-tested. They weren't hypotheticals created inside a classroom in a safe, artificial setting far removed from the field. I was taking my show out onto the streets and achieving positive results!

My jury testimony bolstered the software's credibility when they returned a guilty verdict after soundly rejecting the defense's "weapon focus" theory.

It proved to me, though, that it didn't make a difference if the image was hand-drawn or created on a computer. A sound training program could achieve the results law enforcement was looking for.

Since then, I have successfully trained people at many agencies throughout the United States in the development of computer-created composite images.

Law enforcement agencies lacking an artist can develop good composite images. It only requires proper training, a strong desire to learn and a commitment from the software companies.

My belief is that, regardless of the technology you employ, there's never a replacement for the human element -- in this case, the need to conduct an effective interview.

In the end, it's really about what best serves the victim, not about what's more convenient for me. I will always choose best method for the case I am working, whether that's pencil or pixel.

All that matters to me is that the right person goes to jail.

Chapter 8
Justice Done ...

Cops and criminals always seem to make a dangerous and sometimes deadly mix. We spend long careers playing cat and mouse with them in the hope that when it's all over, we can walk away unharmed and leave the danger behind.

In some instances, retirement from law enforcement comes earlier than planned; with bills to pay and families to support, most of those former officers must continue working.

Some are prepared and choose a vocation far from law enforcement. Others stay close to familiar territory and take similar jobs in uniformed security. If they're lucky, such a position allows them to carry weapons to protect themselves. Some of these jobs require working with large amounts of cash, and they must have a means of protecting themselves.

Even while working dangerous territories, some security jobs become routine and breed complacency. Crooks recognize this and target uniformed couriers, attacking them with deadly frequency. These days, armored car drivers and ATM couriers are becoming the most frequent targets of violent robberies.

As police officers, we vary our daily routine as a matter of safety. Armed couriers and drivers cannot because they have schedules to honor and routes they must follow. Their daily habits make them easy robbery targets. And crooks are more sophisticated than ever before. They conduct surveillance and spend long hours planning, allowing them to execute robberies with deadly efficiency.

In prison, many talk about committing these types of crimes and learn from other inmates how to carry them out. Others are part of organized street gangs that carry out robberies as a gang initiation ritual, or they're "soldiers" carrying out the particular gang's financial business.

The most dangerous crook of all is the independent. He's the thug who wants a quick payoff, an old-school convict or a "three-striker" who has no desire to go back to prison. Conditioned to have little or no regard for human life, he serves no one but himself.

But, as I said at the beginning of the chapter, crooks and cops are a dangerous and sometimes deadly mix. Many times, it's the former cops who wind up having the deadly confrontations with criminals.

In one particular case, the confrontation resulted in the abduction and murder of a former police officer working as a security guard.

Robert T. Walsh, age fifty-nine, was a retired Fullerton police officer whose career was cut short due to knee injuries suffered while doing what he loved most, catching crooks. One of his former colleagues, retired Police Chief Philip Goehring, described him as someone you could always depend on. He said that Walsh had a "stellar" reputation and was "very, very savvy," using his "wisdom and experience to get the job done without having to be aggressive."

After retiring, he found his way to Wells Fargo Armored Services, where he began working as an unarmed security guard approximately six months prior to his murder.

Goehring said that Walsh never expressed any fear about

his job and didn't feel the need to be armed. He had no desire to confront anyone on his job and from his point of view would be safer not having one. One of his sons later echoed Goehring and said his father would rather try to "talk his way out of trouble."

Still, a former employee trained by Walsh later reported he saw him wearing a two-inch revolver concealed in an ankle holster. His statement was consistent with records showing Walsh was the registered owner of a Smith & Wesson, two-inch, .38 caliber, blue steel revolver.

Walsh's routes took him throughout the Orange County/ Los Angeles areas on what the company characterized as a "low-liability" route.

Along the way, he serviced automated teller machines, collecting cash and checks for later deposit by the bank. He worked alone, driving a small, compact car outfitted with a safe. They said that he would have little, if any, cash and the deposit envelopes would be placed inside his vehicle's safe.

On Friday, April 14, 1995, Walsh failed to come home from work. His family immediately reported him missing to the police. They also called to inform his friend, Goehring, who became immediately concerned for Walsh's safety. Not coming home from work was totally out of character for him.

By that time, Wells Fargo had already begun its own investigation into his disappearance. Walsh's last known stop on his route had been at approximately 3:45 p.m. He last radioed his dispatcher informing her that he'd completed his drop at the Wells Fargo Bank branch on the corner of Tustin Street and Collins Avenue in the city of Orange. He told them that he was en route to his next stop at an Albertson's grocery store in Yorba Linda. He never made it.

Walsh's background was impeccable. When people handling large amounts of cash disappear, the focus immediately turns to them. Employers are quick to suspect an "inside job," fearing they've been burned by an unreliable or crooked employee. However, Walsh was nothing short of an honest, exemplary employee.

His disappearance had an unsettling effect on both his family and employer. They hoped someone would spot his blue/grey Ford Escort and immediately report it to police. It would be difficult for anyone to conceal his vehicle, especially with the name of the company, Wells Fargo Security, emblazoned across the back in red letters.

Walsh's family filed a missing-person report with the Orange Police Department. Detectives were assigned to begin an investigation, but there wasn't much for them to go on. It seemed as though Walsh had vanished without a trace.

During follow-up interviews, detectives learned he was well-liked. Everyone who knew him had favorable things to say about him, including his ex-wife. After completing the standard preliminary investigation there was nothing to do but wait.

Walsh's family, not content to wait, began searching throughout Orange County and on the freeways, looking for the car that would be key to finding him.

On Sunday, April 16, two days after Walsh's disappearance, the Orange Police Department made a grisly discovery after responding to an emergency call of an explosion and vehicle fire in the alley to the rear of a business behind a local strip mall.

The Fire Department responded quickly to extinguish the flames. Police soon learned the vehicle was owned by Wells Fargo Armored Services and was the same vehicle driven by Walsh when he was reported missing.

Inside the vehicle, police found a burned body, later identified by fingerprint comparison as Walsh. Evidence at the scene suggested the killer used an accelerant to ignite the car. The fire had been fast-burning. The Fire Department's quick response thwarted the effort to destroy evidence and made it possible to preserve much of the scene.

Witnesses said they saw a man running from the vehicle about the same time it caught fire. They described him as a "pudgy" white male, approximately fifty years old, 5-foot-10 to 5-foot-11 in height, approximately 180 pounds with gray hair, wearing glasses. The man, who police considered a suspect, had hurriedly run off in a westerly direction. His path was traced later by a Sheriff's Department bloodhound that lost the scent a few blocks away.

Now that police knew Walsh's fate, they were left to ponder why. Was he taken by surprise at his last known stop? Or, was there an armed confrontation he was unable to talk his way out of?

An autopsy and evidence examination was conducted in an effort to answer these questions.

Pathologists determined Walsh suffered blunt force trauma to his head prior to his death. Markings on both sides of his head suggested he was struck with a tool similar to a tire iron. His lack of defense wounds convinced police he had been surprised by his attacker.

Walsh also suffered a fatal gunshot wound to his head. The bullet, possibly from a .38 caliber handgun, entered on the left side and angled toward the back of his head, where the bullet came to rest, causing a fracture to his skull.

Further autopsy results showed that he also suffered significant burns to the lower portion of his body and that some hair fibers were found on his shirt.

Detectives would need to turn back to their eyewitnesses if they hoped to find Walsh's killer. Up until now, they were unable to find conclusive forensic evidence that would help them identify a suspect. They began conducting follow-up interviews with two eyewitnesses who saw the subject in and around the area of the murder.

Detectives approached me and asked if I could work with them to develop a suspect sketch.

A witness had seen the subject inside a nearby fast food restaurant after the murder. Moments later, he saw the man on a pay phone outside, on the same corner where the sheriff's bloodhound lost his scent.

The other witness, a woman, had seen the subject throwing something into the vehicle before it burst into flames.

There was nothing remarkable about these two witnesses.

I would describe them as passive witnesses. Sometimes such witnesses can be difficult to work with because there is less "imprinting" of an event within their memory. Studies have shown higher trauma results in the event becoming more deeply embedded within one's memory. However, if handled correctly, these witnesses can provide police with a phenomenal amount of information.

Now, the only obstacle to overcome was their distance from the suspect and the short time they observed him as he fled the area.

In addition to those difficulties, there was a strong likelihood for conflicting descriptions if the witnesses weren't interviewed properly. Multiple witness interviews demand much concentration and guidance from the interviewer. Often, stronger personalities emerge and attempt to hijack the interview. Eyewitness confidence does not always translate to better identifications. Sometimes the submissive personality has better cognitive skills and can be the better witness. It's up to the police sketch artist to recognize this and exploit an eyewitness' strengths and weaknesses in order to guide the interview to a successful conclusion. There have been many times I've left a multiple-witness interview totally exhausted.

Luckily, these two were a rare commodity. They were

good citizens eager to assist police and share what they saw. They worked well together and actively took part in the interview. In the end, they helped develop a composite sketch that appeared to mirror their first impression: the face of a pudgy, older white man.

Afterward, I turned the sketch over to investigators. The witnesses were satisfied, and I thanked them for their courage in stepping forward and becoming involved.

The sketch was released to the media as investigators braced for a flood of telephone tips. Unfortunately, the sketch failed to develop any promising leads, and soon the case had gone cold.

After ten days, pressure was mounting from all directions to solve the case. Heinous crimes like this didn't happen in Orange, a city with consistently low violent-crime rates. The intense political pressure to solve the case caused detectives to try anything to get the break they were looking for. Since all they had were the eyewitness statements, detectives decided to revisit the sketch and try another artist's version.

Normally, you seek the fresh perspective of another police sketch artist if you gain a new witness with better information than your previous one. That avoids unconscious similarities appearing in the second drawing by using the primary artist again.

Unfortunately, you don't always get early breaks you want either. It becomes a test of patience while detectives review evidence and pursue other leads. The fact that detectives aren't getting the leads they so desperately need isn't necessarily the sketch artist's fault.

My concern was with evidentiary issues and later admissibility. A police sketch is evidence of the eyewitness' statement. It must be preserved like other items of evidence.

Luckily, the other artist they hired to redo the sketch was a friend and colleague. She is a true professional in every sense of the word and among the best in the business. We'd worked together in the past and respected and admired each other's work. She worked hard with these witnesses and had not seen my sketch before completing her own. When finished, her sketch bore many similarities to mine. In the end, it didn't really accomplish much. Despite the new sketch, the investigation into Walsh's slaying remained cold. Not long after that, a new lead detective was brought in.

Detective Matt Miller recently transferred from the narcotics unit into the homicide unit and was immediately tasked with Walsh's homicide. After a long, successful tenure as a narcotics detective, he was perfect for the demands of this investigation. With a fresh perspective and Miller's energy, I knew this case would soon be moving again.

Miller was an experienced detective with an easygoing personality. Widely admired by his peers, his passion for sports and dedication to his family was matched only by his hard work ethic and dedication to duty. Savvy and relentless, he was the perfect match for this case.

He began reviewing the case and the multitude of leads that poured in during the earlier investigation. Although there was minimal evidence, he knew the case was solvable.

First, he sent a teletype to local law enforcement agencies detailed the crime. He began to reorganize the case and look for the more promising leads.

Shortly after he sent the teletype, he was contacted by an investigator with the Orange County Sheriff's Department. She wanted to share information about a suspect she was currently investigating in connection with several robberies. His physical description and criminal background was similar, and she thought he might merit further follow-up by Miller.

Miller obtained color photographs of the man and quickly noticed how closely he resembled both sketches.

Author's sketch is on the left, Poyner's photo is on the right.

The suspect, Bill Poyner, had a previous arrest for bank robbery and was currently on federal parole. His criminal history included several previous armed robberies in Orange. Earlier in his career, he had been dubbed the "Dr. Pepper Bandit." When committing his robberies, he would pretend to be buying a can of Dr. Pepper soda before robbing the clerks.

At the time, he committed the robberies with the help of his half brother. Between the two of them, they were responsible for more than one hundred robberies, stretching from the San Luis Obispo County area south as far as San Diego.

Miller felt that Poyner might also be a good suspect for similar robberies Miller was investigating in and around Orange. A search of his background revealed existing felony arrest warrants charging him with auto theft and violating his federal parole status.

He assembled a photographic line-up and took it to the

witnesses. They selected Poyner's photo from a gallery. Both commented on the "roundness of his face," which was clearly present in both sketches, as being a distinguishing characteristic.

With identifications in place, Miller continued to seek information on Poyner. He learned that he had a girlfriend in Arizona. Reviewing her telephone records, it appeared as if several calls had been made from spots along Walsh's route in a time period before the abduction and murder. From the pattern of calls, it appeared that Poyner had been stalking Walsh.

Poyner also had been identified in approximately twenty robberies in the metropolitan Phoenix area. A detective from the Scottsdale, Arizona, Police Department told Miller that he used the alias "Bill Silver." He added that "Silver" enjoyed tennis, billiards and bowling.

This was important information for the detectives, who felt that if he were still in the area they could use this lifestyle profile to help find him.

Detectives began with bowling. They assembled a list of local bowling lanes that supported league teams. The first one they contacted was a popular bowling lane in Orange.

Their efforts paid off. The week before, "Bill Silver" had joined a league that bowled there. "Silver" had provided them with a local address at a motel nearby in Anaheim.

Miller contacted the Anaheim Police Department for support. They sent over a team of uniformed officers and their SWAT team. Several detectives from the Orange Police Robbery Homicide and Gang Unit assembled at the motel and began a surveillance after the manager confirmed Poyner was a guest there and currently inside his room.

Once all the officers were in place, the manager made a telephone call in an effort to lure Poyner to her office. He left his room and was walking to the office when a team of

Anaheim officers arrested him.

A van he'd been seen driving was found parked at the motel. It had been reported stolen from Arizona and had a stolen license plate from the state of Washington affixed to it.

Search warrants were obtained and served on the vehicle as well as the room where Poyner stayed. Inside detectives located a .38 caliber handgun, a pellet gun, a large amount of U.S. currency, two wigs, a hair-coloring kit and clothing matching descriptions of those used in an earlier bank robbery.

Detectives needed to learn more about Poyner though. An examination of the gun from Poyner's vehicle determined it was not the same as the one that fired the fatal bullet into Walsh. Also, the wigs were not a conclusive match for the fibers found on Walsh's body.

Detectives began to interview Poyner at the same time a press release was issued announcing his arrest.

Poyner was a heavy gambler who favored Las Vegas. His primary motivation for committing his long series of robberies was to support what turned into a habit or what others might call an addiction.

Detectives talked to him for several hours, yet he would never admit to any involvement in Walsh's murder. He told detectives, "You will never link me to this crime."

In the several days and weeks afterward, detectives would be contacted by several people who either knew Poyner or led detectives to others who might also know some information.

A former cellmate of Poyner's came forward after seeing an article in the Orange County Register newspaper. He said the two spent time together at a federal prison in Arizona several years earlier. Poyner would often boast about the robberies he committed and talked regularly about robbing money couriers because he was convinced they had lots of money. He bragged that if he had any problems with a courier he would "kill 'em."

The former cellmate said Poyner would move about to different areas to avoid being identified in his robberies. He said Poyner also favored using disguises. He told his cellmate that Max Factor was the biggest asset a robber could have and that if he ever robbed again, his own mother wouldn't know him.

Although the man never knew if Poyner had actually killed anyone, he said that Poyner talked aggressively and would always threaten people. Poyner frightened several people, including his half brother and former crime partner. He was concerned for his safety because he heard about the murder through an associate. He wanted to help the police capture Poyner, not realizing he was already in police custody.

He talked about their former crimes and how they worked together. He felt that Poyner was working with someone despite his earlier assertion to detectives that, "I never work with anybody." He also talked about Poyner's gambling habit and about how violent he was. He told a story about how he and Poyner had been driving on a Nevada highway a few years back. He said that Poyner was holding a cocked gun in the event they were stopped for a traffic violation. He told him, "If he pulls us over he's dead." He said that Poyner always carried a gun during his robberies.

All of these anecdotes were valuable because of the lack of forensic evidence. They helped detectives weave together a chain of circumstantial evidence to convince the district attorney to file kidnapping, robbery and murder charges against Poyner.

In what was considered to be a boost to their case, detectives spoke to his former girlfriend in Arizona. She spoke about their relationship and how he always would allude to his violent temper, warning her, "You never want to see my temper."

She said that he would disappear frequently, taking her car. He told her he would go to Orange County, where he sold items as part of his security supply business. He talked often of violent confrontations with others. Sometimes he threatened her. Despite the talk of violence and the threats, he would always bring her small, unwrapped gifts including some small teddy bears detectives would use to link him to several Orange County robberies. Before presenting their case to prosecutors, they talked to one last eyewitness. A witness had reported seeing Poyner loitering in the area where Walsh body and his vehicle were found. She had taken her son to his karate lesson a couple of days before and had seen Poyner acting "suspicious" in the area. He was seen both inside the self-serve laundry and inside a vehicle watching a small beauty shop next door, looking nervously about. It wasn't until she saw the news report and photo of Poyner that she realized they were one and the same.

Miller was able to successfully link Poyner to several area armed robberies through witness identification and some hard evidence. He combined this with the circumstantial evidence and eyewitness identification to make the case in Walsh's murder, though being largely built on eyewitness ID made it tenuous at best.

The Orange County Public Defender's Office was charged with defending Poyner in what soon became a death penalty case. Because of the nature of the case, the defense attorneys' best hope was to create reasonable doubt about Poyner's identification. They challenged the identification process from the way the composites were constructed to the witnesses' viewing of the photo and live line-ups. When all of their motions failed, the case was ready to go to trial.

Although I'd previously testified in court many times

before, this time it was different. A person's life was at stake based on eyewitness identification, the most fragile evidence of all. The sketches would figure prominently in the prosecution's case, so I expected a long, protracted battle with the defense.

I thought for sure I was going to get my head handed to me in court. The Public Defender's Office had called a local university professor who was an expert on eyewitness identification. I had already met up with a similar expert in the past, but that was in a robbery case.

When any attorney reaches a level of competence in which they are entrusted with someone's life, you find they are quite passionate about their work. I knew that Poyner's attorney would launch a vociferous defense of his life and I would face vigorous questioning, testing my knowledge and calling my work into question.

I arrived in court to testify, and when I saw his attorney I was relieved. I had encountered her several times over the years and found her to be very fair and professional.

When the time came for me to testify, I braced myself for a series of rigorous questions, only to find I was on the stand for mere moments. The prosecutor only asked me a couple of questions to establish the resemblance to Poyner, while the public defender's questions only seemed to reinforce his position.

I came through it in pretty good shape and despite their expert's testimony, the jury found Poyner guilty of kidnapping and murder. Their tactic of creating reasonable doubt by casting the witness identifications as unreliable failed. A judge later pronounced the sentence and sent Poyner to Death Row.

I'm not sure in today's climate we'd have prevailed in such a case without conclusive forensic evidence or a confession by the crook.

Eyewitness identification has come under increased attacks by defense attorneys and death penalty critics. Recently, there have been numerous cases in which defendants have been convicted solely on eyewitness identification but later exonerated by DNA evidence.

There will always be nagging self-doubt in these kinds of cases. I know they're not taken lightly since many district attorney's offices have established panels of attorneys to review these cases and make recommendations before filing charges.

Should people be tried and sentenced to death solely on the basis of someone else saying they did it? It's a polarizing question, but I think any fair-minded person would say no. Most of us think a life sentence in these types of cases would be sufficient to adequately protect society.

I've found over the years that justice comes in many forms and can be a slow, frustrating process for all involved, but it does comes – eventually.

After sentencing, Poyner was sent to San Quentin State Prison where he took up residence on Death Row. Alone and aging in a place where he'd been long forgotten, he was found dead inside his cell a couple of years later, the victim of an apparent heart attack.

Some may feel cheated that the state didn't get the opportunity to carry out the people's sentence. I didn't care. To me it made little difference. Justice had run her course, and now she was done.

MICHAEL W. STREED

Chapter 9
The 'Cottonwood Pervert'

Sexual predators can be the most cunning and frightening criminals that law enforcement officers are tasked with apprehending.

The sheer brazenness of their crimes, coupled with what is often a high degree of intelligence, make them a dangerous adversary. As their attacks continue unabated, they become emboldened by their success, often refining their skills while sometimes taunting their pursuers or, worse, their victims.

For years, many of these predators were able to elude capture. Others could barely control their lust for sexual violence and left a path of evidence that led police right to them.

But in instances where authorities have no conclusive evidence to work with, detectives were left with nothing more than unpredictable human behavior. Sometimes, though, it's this same behavior that investigators hope to profile, predicting patterns that can lead to an arrest.

In the case of serial predators, this pursuit becomes a high-stakes game of human chess. If not for the sheer determination of detectives who work hard to stop these attacks, many of them continue until the suspect loses control and their behavior explodes into a murderous frenzy.

Sometimes these patterns of crimes begin with nonviolent crimes like theft and burglary. Residential burglaries often become precursors or are directly related to sex crimes. Sometimes the clues of a sexually-related burglary are so subtle, the average officer misses them.

In October 1986, a residential burglary was reported to the Fullerton Police Department. While the residents were away, a suspect broke into the home and took money, helping himself to the family car on his way out. Within a few days, the Santa Ana Police Department would receive a report of an indecent exposure, in which the suspect made his getaway in the vehicle that had been reported stolen in Fullerton.

And that was just the start.

After eight years and dozens of victims, police would finally arrest a suspect responsible for creating a climate of fear across the county. In the end, he was responsible for committing countless burglaries, auto thefts, indecent exposure, sexual battery and rape. During those eight years, girls and women ranging from age twelve into their forties were targeted, stalked and eventually victimized by one of the worst sexual predators in Orange County's history.

Fifteen different police sketches, a criminal personality profile and geographic profile were ineffective in tracking him down.

Despite the evidence gathered, it was dogged police work and a police lieutenant's hunch that stopped the suspect, who was identified as Kenneth George Wade, part-owner of a Temecula billiards parlor. Wade, age forty-five, had been arrested several times before and was a suspect in eighty-six of the above incidents scattered throughout several Orange County cities.

This case is unique because of the span of years his crimes covered and the resources used to bring this predator to justice. There have been few cases I've been involved with during my thirty-five years of law enforcement experience that combined the amount of resources put into place to try to stop him.

It's a frightening case that involved a variety of investigative elements and one strong, determined individual who ultimately made the difference.

During his reign of terror, Wade struck in about a half-dozen cities in Orange County. Throughout the course of the investigation, the Santa Ana Police Department took the lead role in trying to identify and apprehend him. The department is a proactive agency known for its award-winning, innovative anti-crime programs. It also is unique as one of the few law enforcement agencies to rely on civilian employees to handle traditional investigative assignments normally reserved for sworn police personnel.

Linda Faust, a civilian criminal investigator, was assigned to the department's Sexual Assault Unit. She investigated a variety of sex-related crimes and was one of the department's composite image system operators. Faust was the first person to recognize a pattern in many of the sex crimes in her city. Reviewing teletypes from other agencies and sharing information with investigators in other cities convinced her they were all seeking same suspect.

Once a case of this magnitude was identified, most law enforcement agencies would transfer responsibility to a sworn investigator. However, Faust's supervisors recognized her as a competent and tenacious investigator who would be able to organize the vast amount of information that needed to be gathered.

These skills allowed her to keep the case. And as the case continued to build, she became the case agent, a point of contact for other detectives to funnel information through to ensure that it reached everyone.

To properly explain the dynamics of this case, I have

broken the chapter down, covering each element of the case within its own section. When you near the end of the chapter, the elements will come together and you'll come to understand why Wade remained such an elusive predator for so many years.

The Suspect

Kenneth George Wade was born in 1950, and it wasn't long before he began exhibiting behavior that would later land him jail for the rest of his life.

At the age of eight, he began prowling around people's homes, peeping into windows. After a couple of years, he became bolder, and at age ten began entering houses. Once inside, he would steal small items or money. If he were lucky enough, Wade would sometimes find a female resident who was alone showering and would quietly watch.

Wade's parents divorced when he was seventeen, about the time he married his girlfriend. She was pregnant with their son, who also would be named Kenneth.

Soon after his parents' divorce, Wade's father remarried. One afternoon in 1969, Wade returned home and discovered that his father had stabbed his step-mother to death. Wade was so traumatized by what happened that he was hospitalized for a short time.

A month after his release, Wade was arrested for entering a home and attempting to rape the female resident. Charges were never filed because Wade told police that he thought the apartment belonged to a friend and that, even though he fondled the woman, he never intended to rape her.

That brush with the law soon was followed by a series of arrests for narcotics and theft related offenses.

Wade's fascination with illicit sex resurfaced in 1979 when he was arrested for exposing himself in public and soliciting a sex act. This arrest was followed a short time later with another for carrying a loaded firearm.

Arrests continued to dog Wade. In 1990, he was arrested for stealing a car from a carwash. For that crime, Wade was sentenced to two years in prison that ran concurrent with his sentence for a 1986 burglary arrest. In that case, he broke into the apartment of a twenty-one-year-old woman and her twin infants. Wade threatened to kill her and the babies if she screamed, but he left without raping her. His escape was short-lived. Wade's fingerprints were found on a window at the apartment, leading to his arrest and conviction.

Throughout Wade's life, he suffered from alcoholism. He was involved in several failed relationships, including three divorces. All of the women described Wade as controlling.

Wade did not have a relationship with his son from his first marriage. The roots of that rejection might have been found in Wade's relationship with his own father. Wade was said to have idolized his father, the owner of a trucking company, who seemed to treat his son with nothing more than disdain. Interviews with those close to Wade said his father hated him and yet would always demand he do things for him, only to later mock and demean Wade.

Throughout his adult life, Wade held a variety of jobs that sustained him over a number of years. He once was a part-owner of a jewelry store with other family members before going on to become an independent jeweler. Later, Wade became a truck driver. At the time of his arrest after the eight-year crime spree, he was managing a pool hall in Temecula.

Those who knew him described Wade as a paradox. Wade was described as one of the friendliest people around. He would always be the first to offer help when people needed it. Others said that even the local police in Temecula knew him and would stop by the pool hall at night and got along with him.

However, diamond merchants and, later, those in the billiard supply business who had transactions with him held a much different view. They described Wade as a ruthless individual who was cold and calculating in his business dealings. One of them colorfully described Wade as a "demanding son of a bitch."

Wade's opinion of himself seemed be one of self-loathing. He survived a suicide attempt after committing one of his earlier rapes and became so disgusted with himself that, later, he would describe scenes where he would stand in front of the mirror at night, staring at himself, screaming at his reflection to stop raping.

After his arrest, Wade became desperate not to lose control. He tried unsuccessfully to manipulate Faust, the investigator, during jailhouse interviews by playing "mind games" with her. But Faust was too smart for that, and she knew when to pull back and when to push back. Soon, it became apparent that she was too much for Wade to handle.

The Victims

Wade's victims ranged from their mid-twenties to their mid-to-late forties and were, for the most part, single women. All were white, with the exception of a Hispanic woman he once confronted in an outdoor laundry room. She spoke only Spanish and was able to scream loudly and scare him away.

The women Wade attacked belonged to a wide range of professions. They were bankers, teachers, real estate agents, waitresses, an interior designer and a psychologist. All were strong, professional women whom Wade hoped to control. Many fought back, otherwise many of the crimes could have resulted in tragic circumstances.

M.O.

Wade liked to target multi-unit condominiums and garden-style duplexes close to freeways with fence-enclosed patios. These styles of multi-unit complexes were plentiful in Orange County. This made it difficult for police to predict where he might strike next.

Once Wade identified targets, he entered his victims' residences through unlocked front doors and windows.

There were instances in which he had to force open a locked door, but usually his victims left their residences unsecured.

Another part of Wade's M.O. that was difficult to predict were the days and times he was most likely to attack. Most criminals are creatures of habit and have an established pattern for committing crime -- but not Wade.

Wade struck all seven days of the week at various times. Sometimes Wade would strike two to three times in one day. At other times, he would commit a rape in the middle of the night.

His calendar was also scattered in his patterns of attack. Sometimes he would strike again the day after a crime, and other times there would be a two-day gap in between, or sometimes he waited as long as a week before striking again.

Wade would often go on binges, committing several crimes in a single day. He would never stay in one area or city for too long. Wade was always on the move and seemed to attack at random. Wade's intelligence allowed him to stay one step ahead of the police who still had no idea how to catch him.

Resources

Before anyone began to recognize that the same

perpetrator committed this series of crimes, many agencies treated them as separate incidents and produced individual police sketches.

Over the years, the suspect sketches in Wade's crimes began to pile up. All of them, whether drawn by a police sketch artist or produced on a computerized/manual system, bore similar facial characteristics. To the untrained eye, it appeared as if each sketch represented a different suspect.

These sketches were released primarily within the law enforcement community, so there was little chance that the public would see them and become confused.

The sketch depicted below was one that I created later during Wade's crime spree. It bore a strikingly similar appearance to Wade, but it had nothing to do with his identification and capture.

Author's sketch is on the left, Wade's photo is on the right.

I created the sketch based on information from a victim of a sexual battery in Orange. During the interview, the woman was very detailed. She was angry, too. When Wade came into her house naked and confronted her, she thought about her three-year-old child standing beside her in the dining room. Wade came up behind the victim as she talked on the phone and reached around, grabbing her breast from behind. She fought back and yelled at Wade to leave her house. He quickly left and was able to escape as she dialed 911.

Faust did another composite image using a computer software program. She was good at interviewing eyewitnesses and knew the software well. Her composite image also bore a striking resemblance to Wade.

Even though there were so many sketches of Wade floating around, no one probably would have associated them with him. Wade had already moved to Temecula, in Riverside County, so there was little chance anyone in Orange County would have remembered him. And it has highly unlikely back then that the image would have spread beyond Orange County anyway. So, despite law enforcement's best efforts, Wade remained free to continue his attacks.

When the sketches failed to generate any useful leads, it was time for detectives to try a different angle.

Detectives thought it would be useful to try generating a criminal profile. Through the FBI, many larger municipal and county law enforcement agencies were able to train their own personnel as criminal profilers. For years, the FBI's highly successful Behavioral Sciences Unit worked on some of the world's most notorious serial killer and sexual predator cases. Now, they were training others in their methods.

As Wade continued to paralyze communities in fear through his continued attacks, John Yarbrough was busy studying the rapist's victims and his method of operation.

As a sergeant with the Los Angeles County Sheriff's Department, Yarbrough routinely analyzed serial crimes and offenders, preparing criminal investigative analysis reports not only for his agency but also for those of surrounding jurisdictions.

These reports were a synopsis of many elements of the

crimes and their victims. More importantly, though, it painted a "word picture" profile of the offender's personality and behavior patterns that might help police focus on probable suspects.

In his report, he painted a chilling picture, describing the rapist as having low self-esteem and self-perceived inadequacies. Yarbrough saw the suspect as a person who was intelligent, but who felt little or no long-lasting remorse for the crimes he'd committed. Yarbrough believed that the suspect was someone who would likely continue committing these crimes until caught. Yarbrough's profile ascribed such traits to Wade as:

- A loner with few, long-term friends.
- A loser, which is how he may choose to project himself.
- Comfortable with nighttime activities with a work history including night jobs.
- A poor dresser.
- Intelligent, contrasted by a poor academic school record.
- Characterized as the "guy next door."
- No longer married or living with a woman.
- Nonathletic in terms of playing team sports, though he might be a jogger.
- Might be the product of a single parent household.
- Probably a convicted felon because of the four-year lapse between crime series.

The profile further described the suspect's sexual crimes against women as not being born from hatred for women as much as from the need to reassure his own ego and sense of masculinity.

This would be helpful to police who were hunting for Wade. Criminal personality profiling has worked in many cases and was popularized in the movie "Silence of the

Lambs" and then on the television series "Criminal Minds." While conducting research on this case, I spoke to retired FBI criminal profiler and Special Agent Roy Hazelwood. He was part of the first group that comprised FBI's famed Behavioral Science Unit, and he specialized in sexual predators. Hazelwood has written many journal articles on the subject of rape and sexual deviancy and has co-authored two popular books, "The Evil That Men Do" and "Dark Dreams," which profile his career and many of his cases.

During the years Hazelwood spent studying sexual predators, he personally interviewed forty-one incarcerated serial rapists who were collectively responsible for raping in excess of 800 women.

Some of these cases are highlighted in his above-mentioned book "The Evil That Men Do." I spoke to Hazelwood and provided him information about Wade's crimes. While he's accustomed to having more complete material when evaluating a case, he was nonetheless able to detail his impressions about Wade.

Hazelwood described Wade as a "Power Reassurance Rapist" who transitioned to a "Power Assertive Rapist." He felt that, based on the information I provided him, Wade was transitioning to an "Anger Rapist" and had been captured just in time before he could injure any of his victims.

Hazelwood evaluated Wade's erratic behavior and the sporadic manner in which his crimes were committed. It was Hazelwood's opinion that Wade was acting impulsively because his crimes seemed to involve little or no planning.

He also believed Wade selected apartment complexes because they afforded him a ready pool of victims and made it easy for him to select his female targets.

Hazelwood told me Wade primarily fit the profile of what he described as a "Ritualistic Offender." This type of offender can have complex fantasies and will engage in what Hazelwood described as "criminal foreplay" with his victims, using them as props to establish a connection with them.

In his article "The Sexually Violent Offender: Impulsive or Ritualistic?" Hazelwood and his co-author, Janet I. Warren, from the University of Virginia, break down the characteristics between the two.

When Hazelwood talks about the criminal behavior of the Ritualistic Offender, he describes their core sexual behavior as being verbal, physical (force) and sexual. He further stated that fantasies play a major role in that type of offender's crimes as they provide a conscious, repetitious template for his multiple crimes.

Yet, to the end, Wade tried to be the good guy and reverted back to his Power Reassurance Rapist characteristics by pleading guilty in court, sparing his victims from testifying and reliving the trauma of his attack.

After reading Yarborough's profile and Hazelwood's assessment of Wade, I think both profilers were spot on in their evaluations of Wade.

Another useful took that Faust used was geographic profiling.

That profiling method was successfully used in serial rape and murder cases investigated in Canada by Constable Kim Rossmo. Rossmo was assigned to the Crime Prevention Unit of the Vancouver Police Department in British Columbia. The method involves determining location and spatial relationships shared by the victim and offender. Often this process can be used to narrow an area where a suspect lives or works.

In Wade's case, geographical profiling didn't work as well as they hoped because Wade was what Rossmo would describe as a "poacher," an offender who travels a distance from another area to commit his crimes.

But it still provided detectives with useful information they could apply to their case.

The detectives made valuable use of these resources. All three -- facial composites, criminal profiling and geographical profiling -- are valuable tools that could be used together or independent of one another. Even though none of them worked out, the fact that detectives had enough imagination to use them was impressive. When any one of the three work the way it is designed, it becomes a powerful tool that can cut considerable time from an investigation and save people from being injured or killed.

The Crimes

In most instances, Wade entered the types of residences he favored through an unlocked sliding glass door. Once inside, he confronted his victims and would begin masturbating his sometimes erect penis as he taunted them by saying things like, "Come get some of this," "Do you want some?" or "I know you want this." In one case, he encouraged the victim to report him, telling her, "Go ahead and call the police, it turns me on!"

This became a consistent pattern of Wade's, trying to create a climate of fear and control. He was so determined that, in one instance, he burglarized a home in the same area of this previous attacks and, finding no one home, used the resident's Polaroid camera to snap a photo of his penis, which he which he left behind the victim's couch so she would find it upon returning home.

Wade was such a sex-crazed degenerate that he would sometimes roam aimlessly about, walking naked, except for a ball cap and tennis shoes, between apartment buildings in his preferred target areas. During his walks, he was on high alert for potential victims, his eyes darting back and forth between windows as he masturbated for any woman who happened to glance out their bedroom window.

But if Wade met too much resistance, or if the women threatened to call the police, he would flee, escaping before police arrived.

Most of Wade's crimes occurred in Orange, on Cottonwood Street on the city's north side. He appeared in the area with such frequency that the residents dubbed him "the Cottonwood Pervert."

Wade liked to vary his pattern of attack, however, and he would soon shift areas, mostly to the south side of Orange, where there was a community of garden-style apartments he preferred.

As Wade's attacks continued, police could see that he was becoming more erratic and increasingly aggressive. In Orange, where he physically attacked two of his victims, one was the women who assisted me with his sketch. In her case, he entered her residence unnoticed and grabbed her breast while she was in her kitchen, talking on the phone.

In the other physical attack, he entered a residence, pushed the woman down onto her couch and held her there. The woman fought back and only narrowly escaped being raped. Wade panicked as he tried to quiet her down, telling her, "OK, OK, be quiet and I'll leave."

Oftentimes, on his way out the door, he would take a little something for himself, like money or small jewelry items.

Detectives from several cities that surround Orange were experiencing similar crimes. Police reports began to pile up in Santa Ana, Placentia, Fullerton and Anaheim. The suspect descriptions bore similarities to the man who was attacking women in Orange: white, in his thirties, average height and weight, with a moustache, wearing a baseball cap and glasses.

The fact that the suspect descriptions were so similar was

unsurprising, as Wade did little to disguise his appearance outside of always wearing a baseball cap and eyeglasses. In fact, he was so careless, that sometimes he would return to the same area and expose himself again to previous victims.

He always had an escape vehicle waiting nearby. In the case for which I completed a police sketch, Wade had practically parked his vehicle near the back door of his victim's residence.

Wade would later tell detectives he used stolen cars that he could easily stash in the large apartment complexes where he used to live. When he moved to Temecula, parking was so limited, he stopped stealing cars. He found that it was easier to steal license plates that he would affix to his own cars to avoid detection.

In 1989, Orange County's female residents got some relief when Wade was arrested for burglary and auto theft and went to prison for four years. After his release in 1993, he began committing crimes again.

The Rapes

Wade committed at least eighteen reported rapes during his rampage. There were probably an equal number that went unreported, so we will probably never know the extent to which he terrorized women.

Of all the rapes reported, it was my opinion that two of the most disturbing reports occurred in August 1994 in Santa Ana and in January 1988 in Anaheim. It should be noted that the rape in Santa Ana was the only known time that any of his victims suffered visible injury.

In that incident, Wade entered the victim's bedroom at about 1:00 a.m. He sneaked into her bed, clamped his hand over her mouth and held a knife against her throat. Calling her by name, he warned her not to scream. He reminded her that he could have killed her already if he wanted to. Wade warned her that she would be all right as long as she followed his directions.

The victim told Wade that she was feeling sick and needed to go to the kitchen for a glass of water. Wade grabbed a handful of her hair and led her to the kitchen with the knife pressed against her back.

When she finished and they returned her to the bed, Wade climbed on top of her and straddled her hips. Wade asked her how long it had been since she last had sex and if she enjoyed it.

The victim tried to persuade him not to rape her by saying she hadn't had sex because of a female problem that required surgery. Wade countered by saying that suggested he had been sent to her for a reason.

She then tried telling him that her family would be returning home soon. But that only caused him to ask if he should hurry his attack and finish. When Wade decided to complete his assault, he told her to keep her eyes closed. He then asked her if she wanted vaginal or anal sex with him. The victim told him that she preferred not to be raped anally, so he forced her legs apart and vaginally raped her.

Wade directed the victim to tell him how big his penis was and how much she enjoyed him "fucking her." She refused, though, and he digitally penetrated her anus before climaxing.

After Wade finished his attack, he put the telephone on her chest and warned her not to do anything for at least five minutes. Wade also warned her not to call the police because he would be watching and would come back again later.

Before Wade left, he stopped to taunt her, saying that she "messed up" by leaving her window open.

When she was sure Wade had left, the victim found that he had taken her purse from where it hung on the bedroom door and moved it into another bedroom, scattering the contents across the bed. She saw that her identification was in plain view and that he had stolen $20. It wasn't until later that she discovered a small stab wound in her back caused by Wade.

The victim looked around her house and saw the dining room window was open. It was the same window used by a cat burglar who entered her home in August the year before. At that time, the thief took her purse while she was inside the house. She only became aware of the theft when she was notified by a neighbor that her purse was lying in the street in front of her home. Coincidence? Maybe. But it likely showed how Wade carefully selected and stalked his victims.

After Wade's arrest, he told Faust that he didn't know that the victim had been stabbed. The investigator noted that Wade almost seemed upset that it occurred. This was consistent with the victim's statement in which she told police that she couldn't remember how she got stabbed either.

The rape case in Anaheim was similar. Like the sexual assault in Santa Ana, Wade entered the victim's bedroom in the middle of the night. He clamped his hand over her mouth as he placed a pillow over her head. Initially, she struggled to breathe, but she soon settled down when she was finally able to catch her breath.

It turned out that Wade had raped the same woman the year before inside an apartment in another area of Anaheim. She knew what Wade was capable of so, for her own safety and that of her children, who were asleep in another room, she listened to his every command as he told her, "You know the drill."

Wade directed her to help him insert his penis into her vagina. Within seconds, he ejaculated. Afterward, he explained to her that he raped women because they "wouldn't have him" due to his premature ejaculation problem.

Before he calmly walked through the front door to leave, Wade commented to the victim how much better he liked her new apartment. After he left, she discovered her kitchen window was open, leading her to believe that was how Wade got into her apartment.

During his series of sexual assaults, Wade often tried to treat his victims as if they were a girlfriend. Wade spent time conducting foreplay, kissing them in an attempt to arouse them prior to the rape. Other times he would lie in bed with them after the rapes, and compliment them on their bodies. Wade also gave them security tips and warned them to get better locks and security devices to prevent an attack from happening again.

It was difficult to predict which Wade was going to show up. Each attack brought out a different set of personal behaviors. When the victims fought back, he would become timid and run away. Other times, he dominated his victims by using verbal threats reinforced by the display of a weapon.

Either way, Wade was a dangerous man whom detectives wanted to catch before he killed someone.

Evidence

Wade left little, if any, evidence at his crime scenes. He had learned well from an earlier burglary conviction that resulted from his leaving fingerprints behind. So when detectives checked the scenes of several burglaries attributed to Wade, they didn't find any prints.

Luckily, Wade left a shoe print impression in the dirt outside one rape victim's residence. It was later matched to a pair of Wade's jogging shoes found during a search after his arrest.

Unfortunately, in an unusual development, the most

critical biological evidence -- his semen -- didn't hold much evidentiary value. Laboratory personnel found that Wade was a non-secretor, which occurs in about 20 percent of the population. As a non-secretor, his body didn't secrete blood-type antigens into bodily fluids such as semen, which otherwise would allow experts to determine his blood type.

Wade also had had a vasectomy, so no sperm was present in his semen.

During the time of Wade's crime sprees, DNA testing was in its early stages of development. Crime laboratory technicians were unable to separate his cells from his female victim's white cells, which made DNA typing impossible.

However there were other pieces of evidence that pointed to Wade's involvement.

Wade left two notes inside victims' residences in Santa Ana. They were positively identified as being written by Wade after an examination by a Santa Ana Police Department forensic documents examiner.

And to wrap up the remainder of the evidence, detectives had the police composite sketches that resembled Wade and his identification courtesy of the brave eyewitnesses.

The Capture

Wade's attacks had continued unabated since his release from prison in 1993, and on July 24, 1995, at about 4:35 p.m., he struck again. This time the attack occurred in Anaheim, near the 91 Freeway and Kraemer Avenue.

A woman was inside her garage when Wade approached and grabbed her. Fearing she was about to be raped, she fought back. Consistent with his response many times before when women fought back, he ran away.

About ten minutes later, Wade reappeared in Orange, where he tried to rape another woman. This time, the attack was interrupted by her husband. He watched Wade flee the area, driving away in a small, white compact vehicle. The husband immediately called police and provided them with the vehicle's description and the license plate information. Police learned while researching the license plate that it had been stolen off another vehicle.

Wade still was determined to rape someone, whoever she might be. At about 5:26 p.m., Wade returned to Anaheim. This time he went the opposite direction and drove into a residential tract farther east than his previous two attacks.

When Wade found his target residence, he made entry. By then, Wade had already disrobed and was naked when he entered the home and tried to rape the female occupant. But she decided she wasn't going to let him rape her, so she fought back and hit him across the face with a tape dispenser she was holding in her hand. Once again, when Wade encountered resistance, he fled.

In my experience in law enforcement, having a suspect commit three unsuccessful rape attempts within about an hour was extraordinary. Anaheim police began working the crimes right away. They assigned detectives and a street surveillance team to try locating the suspect. Police had been briefed about the "Cottonwood Pervert's" activities over the years and his habit of returning to an area multiple times searching for victims.

At 9:44 p.m., Anaheim police received a complaint from a resident that she had just been confronted in her garage and followed to her front door by a subject who was masturbating.

Once again, it was Wade, "bingeing," as he roamed randomly about, searching for more victims.

Anaheim Police Lt. Joe Reiss had just briefed his officers before sending them out to conduct saturation patrols in areas where they felt the rapist might return to stalk his victims.

Reiss figured that the rapist might return to the scene

of the day's first attempt, so he drove into the area see if he might show up. As Reiss arrived, he saw a small, white compact car driving toward him. The car had no front plate, but the driver matched the suspect description.

As Wade drove past him, Reiss looked at the rear license plate. It matched the one reported from the earlier rape attempt in Orange.

Reiss made a U-turn and began to follow the car as he informed his dispatchers that he was following the suspect vehicle.

Wade left the area and drove westbound on La Palma Avenue. Reiss followed him until backup units could arrive. When Wade reached Kraemer Avenue, he pulled into a gas station, parked his vehicle and exited.

Reiss pulled up and stopped his police vehicle behind Wade. He jumped out and pointed his duty weapon at Wade, ordering him to raise his hands up to surrender. Wade was slow to comply. He looked confused, as if he were thinking about his predicament.

Suddenly, Wade dropped his hands, jumped back inside his vehicle and drove off at a high rate of speed. Reiss jumped back in his vehicle and began chasing Wade, who tried to escape his pursuers, in a police chase that reached speeds of approximately seventy-five miles per hour.

Wade never stood a chance. The Anaheim Police Department's helicopter joined the pursuit and monitored the chase from above. A helicopter observer radioed Wade's location to officers below as they watched Reiss chase him into a condominium complex on Orange's northern city limits.

Wade desperately snaked his vehicle through the carport area until he reached a dead-end. In a panic, Wade bolted from his vehicle and ran toward a fence. He was able to find a hole in it that was large enough for him to fit through.

Wade came out on the other side and began to run along a trail bordering the Santa Ana River. His escape was short-lived, as Reiss popped out the same hole and continued chasing him.

With Reiss close behind him, Wade kept looking back at him, yelling, "I don't want to go back to prison!"

After chasing Wade for several hundred yards, Reiss and another officer caught up with him. They tackled and subdued him, ending the career of one of Orange County's most prolific serial rapists.

Once Wade was in custody, Faust was able to interview him. During her interviews, Wade admitted to many of his crimes. But Wade made the mistake of trying to manipulate Faust, promising her more information if she would keep coming back to jail to visit him. Faust was smart though. Once she had all the information she needed to present a case to prosecutors, she stopped seeing him.

For her efforts, the Santa Ana Police Department awarded Faust its Service Medal. At that time, she was the only civilian to be awarded such a high honor by the department.

Reiss later described Wade's arrest as one of the most satisfying of his career.

In the end, Wade surprised everyone by pleading guilty to thirteen felony charges. The judge accepted his plea and sentenced him to a prison term of sixty years to life.

Wade was sent to prison, where he later died.

No longer able to menace his victims, or anyone else for that matter, now all that is left is the memory of the pain Wade caused. Sometimes I think that's more horrible than the man himself.

Chapter 10
His Name Is 'Anthony'

Beaumont is a small city of approximately 11,000 residents located in eastern Riverside County, approximately seventy-seven miles east of Los Angeles.

Interstate 10 cuts a lazy path through the center of town. This asphalt trail stretches from the beaches of Santa Monica eastward through Middle America. With its rolling hills and picturesque mountain views, Beaumont is a snapshot of American innocence.

Young families flocked to the area to nestle into a quieter life, hoping to feel a sense of community and to insulate themselves from the ills that plagued their urban neighbors. So while parents worked, their children played.

Thriving in this idyllic setting, residents had no clue that on April 4, 1997, their innocence would be shattered forever. The community's tranquility would be replaced by mournful calls for help that were heard around the world after residents learned a stranger had stolen one of their children.

The child's name was Anthony Martinez, a ten-year-old who was abducted at knifepoint while playing in his front yard with his brother and a cousin.

Until that day, Anthony's mother, a lifelong Beaumont resident, considered it a safe place to raise her family, with the same small-town lifestyle she experienced growing up.

She described Anthony as a wonderful son who was independent and mature for his age. He was always concerned about time and was always punctual. His mother also shared that Anthony always looked out for others. He was the kind of child who would gladly offer his lunch money to kids who didn't have any food. He also liked to share his personal possessions.

Anthony was inquisitive about the world around him. He was a happy and intelligent child, always asking questions about the Bible and about things that went on around him.

A week before his abduction, Anthony's mother said they spoke about how to recognize the difference between a "stranger" he just might not know and someone who was dangerous. She tried to explain the difference in the best terms possible, cautioning him to use his own judgment, urging him to trust his own instincts.

Yet, despite the safety measures she instilled in her children, she also kept track of where they were at all times. And when they would move to another location to play, they would always tell her first.

She was home while the boys played in the fenced front yard of a next-door neighbor and a stranger approached.

The man struck up a conversation with the boys as he tried to coax them closer to the fence. From a distance, he asked them if they could help him find his cat. He showed them a photograph of a cat and offered them money for their help in finding it. The cat, a beautiful calico, was seated on a chair in the living room of a home that looked warm and comfortable, much like their own.

Curious but wary, the boys edged close enough to the fence to get a quick look at the photo. Staying beyond arm's reach, the fence offered them additional protection from the stranger.

Somehow, the man was able to convince them to leave the safety of the yard to help him. They ventured into an alley that ran along the set of houses, a mere twenty feet from the safety of Anthony's home.

The man suddenly turned violent as he brandished a knife at them and made a grab for Marco, Anthony's younger brother.

To protect Marco, Anthony unselfishly placed himself between the stranger and his brother.

Turning his focus to Anthony, the stranger reached out and grabbed him as the other children looked on in horror. He put Anthony in a headlock and carried him to a vehicle parked nearby.

Anthony bravely fought the entire way to the vehicle, kicking and screaming as he desperately tried to attract the attention of someone, anyone, who could help him escape.

All his brother and cousin could do was watch helplessly as the kidnapper drove away with Anthony. Marco stood frozen while his cousin ran back to Anthony's house screaming in terror.

Anthony's mother heard the screaming outside. She said the child was so hysterical, it took adults a full fifteen minutes to calm him to learn exactly what happened.

Once they learned that Anthony had been kidnapped, an emergency call was made to the Beaumont Police Department. Officers who responded interviewed the children and confirmed that a crime had occurred. What followed was a frantic search for Anthony and his kidnapper as police mobilized more resources, expanding their search to a wider area.

The abduction of a child by a stranger is a terrifying crime that no community or police agency can ever fully prepare for.

Schools teach students about stranger danger, and

parents talk to their children to reinforce the message at home. I remember, when I was much younger, the "stranger danger" was always characterized or lampooned as a "dirty old man," naked underneath a long raincoat – not much more than a harmless flasher who accosted women and children for the shock value more than anything else. Today, that has all changed.

It's even difficult for the police to quantify what children should look out for these days. Child predators come from all walks of life and don't necessarily have a signature "look." All law enforcement can do is try to develop procedures for reacting quickly to reports of child abductions. Many police agencies work in cooperation with community groups and nonprofit agencies to help identify resources they can use in these difficult investigations.

The fear and hysteria these crimes cause is understandable because time is an enemy that works against the safety of the child. Statistics show that nearly 70 percent of children taken by a stranger are murdered within the first three hours after the crime occurs.

FBI statistics showed that in 2014, there were approximately 466,949 reports of missing children entered in the National Crime Information Center computer system. That's about as many people as live in Long Beach, California.

Not all of the missing child cases involve stranger abductions. Children disappear for a variety of reasons, including abductions by a family member like an estranged parent.

In 1997, when Anthony was kidnapped, the California Department of Justice reported 81 abduction cases throughout the state that did not involve a family member but were committed by a stranger.

These situations are extremely dangerous for a child

because the abductor has a strong motivation not to allow their victims to survive and become a witness.

Unlike an abduction committed by a family member, the kidnapper in a stranger case does not share the same familial bond with the child and can easily depersonalize the child, making it easy to harm to them.

Law enforcement officers, on the other hand, take these cases *very* personally. Most of us have children and can sympathize with the heartbroken parents of abducted children. That is why they easily spend long, frustrating hours working these cases with the single-minded goal of bringing these children home safely.

With a family of my own, I understood this all too well. Like most parents in the area, my wife and I were too busy on that day to have any idea about the frantic search for Anthony that was taking place less than an hour's drive away. Back then, there were no Amber Alerts to light up your cellphone, no loud alert tone to interrupt your favorite television program and no lighted billboards to draw your attention while driving down the freeway.

Today, it is nearly impossible *not* to be aware of a child abduction, and that's a good thing. Public awareness is key in such situations. The more eyes out looking increases the chances of the child being found safely.

I was alerted to Anthony's kidnapping by a Saturday morning phone call. A special agent from the California State Department of Justice was on the line. He took a moment to brief me on the situation and wanted to know if I was available to come to the Beaumont Police Department to sketch a kidnapping suspect.

I jumped at the opportunity to help and hung up the phone, taking a moment to reflect on the importance of the assignment and what the sketch could mean to Anthony and his family.

I ran upstairs to let my wife know what had happened. I then gathered my sketching materials and stopped to give my own sleeping children a kiss on their foreheads as I barreled out the door, jumped in my car and went racing toward Beaumont.

Less than an hour later, I arrived at the Police Department and was introduced to Pat Smith, Beaumont's police chief. He and his staff invited me to a briefing that was ready to begin, which would provide the latest updates to the investigation.

I walked into their briefing room and was awestruck by the number of uniformed police and investigators who were present. They represented a variety of area law enforcement agencies that were eager to assist, despite the effect the loss of manpower might have on their own communities.

Law enforcement agencies are legendary for their territoriality and often times are reluctant to cooperate with one another, but this time it was different. The officers heeded a call for mutual aid and the desire to find a young boy whose spirit was felt throughout the room.

After the briefing, I was introduced to agents from the FBI and the California Department of Justice. They thanked me for coming as I brushed aside their praise for my work in previous cases. They briefed me about the witnesses I would be meeting as I was led me to a small interview room where I set up my drawing equipment.

A few moments later I was introduced to the two brave boys, who were still shaken from the experience of seeing their brother and cousin being carried off in a violent confrontation with a stranger.

I soon realized that a conventional interview would not be appropriate here. So, while the agents sat in semi-comfortable chairs, the kids and I hit the floor. I lay down, sat cross-legged or kneeled, as I turned myself into a benevolent contortionist who needed every trick and technique to get a good sketch from these boys.

Most children describe things as shapes and, if allowed, will gladly draw you a picture if you let them.

They can identify people and pictures and are probably more adept at showing rather than telling you because of the limitations of their language skills. In most cases, children are truthful in their description of a person or events. That's not to say that they cannot be led or coached by adults, and the thing I worry most about in such cases is them trying to please me so much so that the drawing becomes more my own interpretation than theirs.

Of course, there are different tricks you can use, like testing their description by feigning confusion and asking them to explain several different times, or showing them a reference photo of something totally different than what they are describing.

The thing of course I like most about interviewing children is that their minds are not cluttered with biases that adults collect over the years.

They also are pretty good at simplifying things. For example, take a chair. A child might tell you that it is an object with four legs that you sit on with a back on it. They may add color or something else they observe.

An adult, on the other hand, might go on and on about the color being tacky, the material being a texture they don't care for and the chair back being uncomfortable.

Suppose this chair was missing a leg or a support spoke was broken out of the chair back. By the adult cluttering the description with their own biases you might be looking for the wrong chair because important identifying characteristics were left out – like the obvious, a leg was missing. They're too busy telling you what they don't like about the chair rather than giving you the proper description about its appearance.

This simplified description illustrates the differences

between the ways children approach their observations versus the way in which adults do.

Throughout my career, I have found my two most significant obstacles when interviewing people for a sketch are keeping a child's interest and keeping adults focused.

To illustrate how good a child witness can be, let me relate a 1992 case in which I was asked to draw a sketch for the San Bernardino Police Department.

A five-year-old child was walking to school with a friend when a car pulled up curbside. The driver tried to abduct the boy, who escaped unharmed. The suspect was described as a youthful looking African American man with a "fade" Afro hairstyle and a distinctive cleft in his chin. His vehicle, a Saturn, with an unusual green-colored paint, was equally distinctive.

A couple of months after the incident, the child was riding in a car with his mother when he saw a similar vehicle. The driver matched the description, and they copied down the license plate. They reported it to the police, who tracked down the vehicle and obtained a photo of the driver. Although the child positively identified the driver of the Saturn as the same man who tried to abduct him before, the District Attorney's Office was reluctant to prosecute solely on the identification of a lone, five-year-old witness.

Looking at the sketch, though, and comparing it to the suspect's photo -- the case was a testament to the ability of a young child to accurately identify a person involved with a crime. The sketch was dead-on accurate.

In Anthony's case, over the first couple of hours I spent with the children, I asked them to remain calm and remember what they could about the events of the previous day. I asked them to recall the nightmarish image of the abductor so I could record it and turn the world loose on him. We worked tirelessly, unaware of the media storm that was brewing outside.

I remember these boys as good witnesses who did everything asked of them. Details of the abduction and a description of the kidnapper began to emerge as the agents and I listened intently. I find it helpful to have investigators present sometimes in the event some fresh information is disclosed that requires immediate follow up.

The only thing that kept breaking my concentration was an investigator who would pop his head inside the room from time to time to ask when the drawing was going to be finished. The media outlets were growing impatient and were anxious to release the sketch.

The constant interruptions began to get annoying. The importance of a timely completion was not lost on me, but I don't work for the media and my interview sessions weren't scheduled to coincide with the evening news. I realized though, in a case like this that the media's full cooperation is vital.

I also knew that with a life possibly hanging in the balance that the need to get an accurate sketch, no matter how long it took, was most important of all. When we finally completed the drawing, I remember showing it to them.

I listened broken-heartedly as Anthony's brother looked at the sketch and hung his head, blankly staring at the floor and kept repeating a wish we all shared: "I just want my brother back."

I hung around afterward long enough to talk to the chief and his investigators before leaving, and I was able to sneak around the media crush as I was leaving.

A news reporter did catch up with me a few days later to ask me how I felt about everybody in the world seeing my sketch. I told her it felt great because if we ever hoped to catch this guy it would require the whole world seeing it.

The sketch achieved its desired effect, as several leads

began to pour in. By the time the case reached its peak, over 30,000 leads had been received that required follow-up.

Before following up any leads, the police first like to clear family members off the list of potential suspects. Once that is done, the investigators begin to look at the next class of suspects: registered sex offenders, particularly ones who have a record for child molestation.

Some might consider that unfair, but let's face it -- people who commit these types of crimes usually have a previous criminal history. If not crimes against children, then they've had some other run-in with the law.

So, while the authorities went about their search for Anthony's killer, I went back to business and continued with my life catching other crooks and raising a family. But I remained committed to following the progress of the case.

Ten days after Anthony was abducted came the heartbreaking news. His body had been found in the desert, about twenty miles away from his home.

A park ranger located the body after seeing vultures circling overhead. When he went to the spot, he found the body of a young boy. He was nude with his hands tied behind his back and his legs secured with duct tape. The killer made no attempt to hide the body, leaving it in the open.

People were thunderstruck. I think everyone had held out hope that as long as Anthony's body was not found, he might still be alive.

Now, the investigation and manhunt intensified, and new resources were tapped. One day my son, watching the television news, asked me what had happened to my sketch. When I asked why, he said they had showed a different one on the news a few moments before.

I telephoned the Riverside FBI office and asked the special agent in charge what had happened. He said that new witnesses had been found, adult witnesses, who had seen a similar person in the downtown area loitering before the abduction. The investigators felt these new witnesses would be more reliable than the children who were there at the time of the abduction.

He said that they were getting intense pressure from a popular crime-fighting television show whose producers were pressuring them to use an artist they had hired. To avoid outside interference, the FBI flew in one of their own artists from the Visual Information Unit in Washington, D.C., to work with the adult witnesses.

I wasn't pleased, but I understood their desire to solve the case. What I will never understand is why these trained investigators didn't have enough sense to trust the people who had been there – those terrified children. I had enough experience to feel that they were heading in the wrong direction, but it wasn't my call. I just had to swallow my pride and hope for the best.

I had long suspected that there was posturing going on behind the scenes. The Beaumont Police Department had the abduction, the FBI was assisting but at times seemed to be running the show, and now the Riverside County Sheriff's Department had the murder case.

The question now was, whose responsibility was it to bring this killer to justice?

Luckily, these agencies were smart. They wisely put together a task force to pool their resources and avoid the kind of interagency bickering that can stall and derail an investigation. They knew that if they were to find Anthony's killer, they must do it together.

Over the next four years, the community began to heal. Anthony's parents dealt with their pain and the realization that, although Anthony was gone, they still had a family to raise.

Although the case itself was never closed, the task force

was pared down over time as frustration set in over the lack of an arrest.

Officers and investigators went back to regular assignments, and the investigation was quietly turned over to the Riverside County Sheriff's Department, which assumed the lead role.

I was contacted by a detective from that department when the four-year anniversary of Anthony's abduction and murder was coming up. He said that impending date had launched a new push to re-establish the case in the public's consciousness. A press conference and media blitz were planned. I told him that I thought it was a great idea because I believe that most of these cases can be solved. I was eager to help in any way I could.

I listened intently as the detective summarized what steps had been taken in the case up so far. I had worked with the Riverside County Sheriff's Department many times before and found them to be a professional agency. They had pored over the case again and re-interviewed the witnesses.

After careful review, they felt that the sketch I had done, previous to the one the FBI developed, was a more accurate rendition. They wanted me to make some changes that the other witnesses recommended, such as opening the shirt collar because my original depicted it buttoned to the neck, and they liked the style of ball cap from the FBI sketch better.

By this time in my career, I was able to do some pretty significant work using computer imaging. Although I refused to abandon my pencil in favor of software, there were instances such as Anthony's case in which the two could be successfully merged.

First, I scanned both sketches into a computer and placed them side by side on the monitor for closer evaluation. Now I could properly visualize what the eyewitnesses were talking about. I was able to redraw the FBI artist's ball cap in my own drawing style and use the software to seamlessly merge it into my drawing as if it were an original.

It looked much better now, but I still had the issue of the collar.

Unless there is something distinctive about clothing, I don't normally include it. I always include necks, though, because I don't like depicting heads that look like they are floating aimlessly about the page. I included it this time only because of the magnitude of the case and I figured anything and everything might be helpful. However, we ultimately decided that it was too much of a distraction, so I airbrushed it off.

In the end, this updated sketch was a result of input from the young witnesses who were there and watched Anthony get kidnapped.

The most distinctive physical attribute this suspect possessed was what were described as "piercing" blue eyes. The black and white sketch I had done depicted an intensity in the suspect's gaze without the effect of color.

Once I transmitted the drawing to investigators, they took a couple of days to review it. They later came back and said that, although the witnesses were satisfied with it, they wanted to try a colorized version.

Under normal circumstances, color would not be recommended. Colors are hard to accurately match and degrade each time a sketch is reproduced. Sometimes people take sketches too literally, and color can thus be confusing. But I am not opposed to using it if that is what the police agency wants. In this case, since the eye color was the dominating color issue, I was willing to give it a try.

The trick to reproducing a drawing is not losing the image's integrity during the transfer. To help keep the spirit of the original drawing, I made a smaller print of my completed drawing and projected it on a piece of toned paper. Tracing the outline and filling in the features, I was able to lay down color using colored pencils. I was successful in maintaining the image integrity as the colorized version matched the black and white version. The blue eyes came out looking pretty intense. Thanks to the eyewitnesses' description, I was successful in capturing his dominating physical feature. We also agreed that a neckline would be helpful, and an open-collared Pendleton-style shirt was added.

The plan was to enlarge the image and place it on a billboard in the area off the Interstate 10 freeway where Anthony's body was found, in such a way that the suspect's face would stare down on passing motorists.

As a result of renewed media coverage on the four-year anniversary of Anthony's death, several new leads were generated. But despite all the attention and advances in DNA technology, the 1997 case remained unsolved.

On Feb. 26, 2002, the investigation received a boost when it was reported that the Denver Police Department was investigating an abduction of two young girls, ages five and eight. They were able to provide police with a sketch that bore a resemblance to Anthony's abductor.

The abductor in this case lured the two girls into his vehicle while they were returning home from school. He asked them for assistance in finding his "lost puppy." He later tricked them into drinking alcohol while at a motel or apartment complex. It was unknown if they were sexually assaulted, but they were later dropped off alive.

One was located at a store, while the other was found by the side of the road, crying.

Although the sketches shared a similar appearance, investigators didn't believe they were the same person.

I was confident that one day the case would be solved. Advances in scientific evaluation of evidence coupled with good old-fashioned police work can do much to solve cold cases.

It was always my belief that somebody knew something out there though and for some reason was either afraid or unwilling to turn in a friend or a loved one. Yet, many years had passed since an innocent boy had been murdered to satisfy insatiable lust or anger, and I don't understand why anyone would hesitate to call the police.

But, luckily there was still hope. Two important pieces of information were released to the public that could help identify Anthony's killer. One was my updated sketch, and the other was a criminal behavior profile.

Criminal profilers do amazing work by painting a word picture of the offender that in this case, would help support the suspect's physical appearance. After all, murdering someone, especially a child, is an aberrant behavior and a criminal act that is not always easy for someone to adjust to and hide. There are visual clues available that people need to notice.

The first clue is the suspect sketch.

The latest sketch was created after extensive interviews with eyewitnesses, family members and a re-evaluation of reported sightings. Detectives believe the updated sketch to be a more "realistic" depiction of the suspect who was described as a white man, approximately twenty-five to thirty-five years old, 5-foot-8 with a thin build, brown moustache and "piercing" blue eyes.

At the time of Anthony's abduction, the suspect was wearing a long-sleeved red, white and black plaid shirt, blue jeans and a dark blue baseball style cap. He also might have had a six-month-old German shepherd-mix dog named Buster with him.

Eyewitnesses also reported the suspect fleeing the abduction in a white sedan with red pinstriping.

Another important clue was the criminal personality

profile that detectives requested from FBI behavior analysts, commonly referred to as criminal profilers. They evaluated the crime scene and other reported information, making it possible for them to make observations about the unknown suspect. Their detailed analysis included:

- A likely change or alteration of his personal appearance at or near the time of the initial abduction.
- A noticeable increase in the use of illicit drugs and/ or alcohol.
- A sudden change in work schedule and/or habits.
- The disposal or alteration of his white sedan automobile.
- An unusual interest in this case, which might manifest as a tendency to continually talk about it or follow the investigation in the media.
- The suspect's abrupt departure from the area for what could be a believable excuse, such as to attend to matters concerning the death of a family member, to go on an unscheduled vacation, etc.

Much attention had been given to this case. An army of police, modern science and community resources were mobilized, appeals to the public made and a substantial monetary reward offered. Despite all that, no suspect was identified as years passed.

For many years after Anthony's killing, I carried a copy of the sketch tucked away inside my day planner. Back then, I always began my days by gazing at the sketch. It fueled my passion and helped remind me of why I continued to push forward through so many heartbreaking cases.

On July 2, 2005, Anthony's case was finally solved after police arrested Joseph Edward Duncan III in the murder of an Idaho family and the abduction and sexual assault of the only surviving family member, a young girl named Shasta

Groene.

Shasta had been rescued after a waitress noticed Duncan enter the restaurant with her. The waitress recognized the girl from news reports and called police. She became a hero when police responded quickly to recover Shasta and arrest Duncan, a serial child predator suspected in the murders of other children throughout the country.

During the investigation that followed, authorities noticed that Duncan resembled my sketch of Anthony's kidnapper. They notified Riverside County sheriff's detectives, who were able to match Duncan's thumbprint with a partial print found on a piece of the duct tape used to bind Anthony.

Author's sketch is center, Duncan's photo is on the left and right.

Now, after convictions and several criminal court proceedings in the Idaho and California cases, Duncan awaits execution in federal prison. And while the court's punishment won't bring Anthony back, it will help ensure that no other child or family suffers at the hands of at least one murderous pedophile, Joseph Edward Duncan III.

Duncan created his own private hell on earth through his misdeeds and the pain he caused several families. But that doesn't mean we have to live in it with him. Society must remain vigilant in our protection of children to make sure this never happens again. It's up to all of us now to take up the fight to protect our children, to protect all children.

I know I am all in. How about you?

Chapter 11
A Lethal Lawyer

I pulled my police vehicle into what would normally be a quiet residential street in Villa Park on May 30, 1997. That day though, it was anything *but* quiet. The sense of peace and security that residents had come to know was shattered by a single gunshot that felled an attractive young homemaker and mother.

Murders were something unfamiliar to the community. The wealthy enclave of approximately 10,000 residents within the city of Orange enjoyed a quiet life of privilege apart from the noisy urban sprawl. Villa Park is considered as close to utopia as you'll ever find. It's a community where people know their neighbors and are spoiled by a nearly nonexistent crime rate. Things like this just did not happen there.

By the time I arrived, the crime scene was already adorned in bright yellow tape. Officers at the scene carefully cordoned off the area to protect any evidence that the killer might have left behind and to keep curious onlookers at a safe distance.

I parked my car and stopped to look around before ducking inside a residence to interview my eyewitness. As I prepared to create a sketch of the murder suspect, sheriff's employees scurried about, setting up portable lights and a mobile command post in anticipation of a long night. Looking around, I couldn't help but notice all the black and white patrol cars and the colorful collection of plain "wrap" detective cars that were parked in every possible angle.

To the casual observer, the crime scene could have been mistaken for a Hollywood film set where they might be shooting a television crime drama. Anything was possible. After all, Villa Park did have a Hollywood connection. Years earlier, actor Kevin Costner attended Villa Park High School, where he was a star baseball player.

But, no, in this case, it was the real deal. There was a killer on the loose, and detectives were waiting with an eyewitness and the expectation that I would come up with a sketch of the killer.

The victim in this case was Janie Pang, age thirty-three. Janie was a Villa Park homemaker reportedly living the good life after marrying Danny Pang, a local businessman, five years before. They moved into a spacious Villa Park residence with their children a couple of years before the murder.

Janie had left behind a life as an exotic dancer and could now spend her time volunteering at her children's school and zealously tending to her rose garden. Sometimes, she would enjoy the afternoon roller-blading through the neighborhood. Those who saw her described Janie as a "stunningly attractive woman who was hard to miss."

The chain of events that led to Janie's murder began at about twelve o'clock in the afternoon. Pang's housekeeper answered a knock at the front door. There she greeted a man with a pencil-thin moustache, dressed in a business suit and carrying a briefcase. The housekeeper told sheriff's detectives that the man -- who was white, in his mid-thirties, about 5-foot-11 -- appeared to be a professional so she didn't perceive anything threatening about him.

The stranger asked if he could see the owner of the residence, so the housekeeper invited him inside while she went to tell Pang that she had a visitor.

Pang returned and had a brief conversation with the man before he pulled out a handgun and began chasing her around the house. As he chased Pang, the panicked housekeeper was able to shuttle Pang's children out the back door to a neighbor's home, where she dialed 911 to summon sheriff's deputies.

Back inside the house, Pang ran upstairs as she tried to escape from the gunman. She went into a bedroom, took refuge inside a closet and closed the door, attempting to hide or to shield herself against an attack.

The stranger quickly followed and fired several shots through the closed closet door, fatally wounding Pang. The man immediately fled the home as Pang lay bleeding to death inside her closet. Alert witnesses saw him leaving the area in what they described as a dark-colored Ford Taurus or Chevrolet Cavalier.

Sheriff's detectives briefed me beforehand and told me that Pang's neighbor had clearly seen the suspect's face. Now, detectives asked me to work with her to produce a composite sketch. With crime scene technicians scouring Pang's home looking for clues, the sketch would be the only evidence they had at that time.

I sat with the witness in the comfort of her living room, and we worked together on the drawing. It wasn't the ideal location due to the constant distractions caused by detectives and others who kept walking through the room. Though it was difficult for the witness to remain focused, we made it work. After working together for a couple of hours, we were finally able to create a composite sketch that she felt strongly resembled Pang's killer.

Looking at the sketch, the witness commented that the gunman's moustache had appeared to have a "theatrical look." To her, it looked like the suspect had glued it on his face. She also remarked on his hair, saying it had a "box-like" shape that was perfectly sculpted with a well-defined part.

When we were finished, I handed the sketch over to sheriff's detectives. Later, it was distributed to the local media where it was aired on television and printed in Los Angeles and Orange County area newspapers

Now that the sketch had gone public, sheriff's detectives began to interview people and search for clues. They quickly eliminated Janie's husband, Danny Pang, as a suspect because he was away on business in San Francisco. But, during the investigation, they learned that Danny Pang owed approximately $20,000 in legal fees to a local law firm for previous work they conducted on his behalf. Detectives at the time did not have any concrete evidence linking this to the murder, but the information itself demanded further investigation.

Authorities learned that Danny Pang's personal lawyer recommended a partner with the law firm because of his expertise in complex securities law. The partner, Hugh "Randy" McDonald, was supposed to receive approximately $4,000 from the total of the legal fees owed to his firm.

Detectives faxed my sketch to the law firm. When they received it, the secretary handed a copy of the sketch to one of the law firm's other partners and commented, "Why are they sending us a drawing of Randy? We have plenty of photos of him."

When detectives heard about the secretary's comment, they began searching for McDonald to determine if he was a viable suspect.

Author's sketch is on the left, McDonald's photo is on the right.

During their attempt to contact McDonald at home, they were met by his wife, who told detectives that he was away on business in San Jose. McDonald had taken a June 5 flight, she said, called her from the airport to let her know that he had arrived safely.

The following morning, McDonald's wife received a surprise package from Federal Express containing family financial documents, the deed to their home and a letter. What she didn't know was that McDonald was planning on staging his own suicide as a ruse designed to give him a head start as he fled to Utah, where he hoped to begin a new life.

As authorities stepped up their search, McDonald was busy scanning newspaper obituaries, stealing names from the dead, to help himself assume new identities. To keep a low profile, McDonald took on several menial jobs to make ends meet. At times, he worked as a meat-plant laborer, a construction worker and even a paralegal.

McDonald eventually took up residence in Salt Lake City, using the name Robert Belmont. In an ironic twist,

McDonald posed as an attorney. It wasn't long before a tipster alerted Orange County authorities that Belmont the lawyer was actually McDonald the fugitive. Detectives rushed to Utah to arrest him only to find that he already fled the area.

The missed opportunity in Salt Lake City started a four-year odyssey as authorities continued their hunt for McDonald, who seemed to have dropped into a rabbit's hole.

As the investigation continued, sheriff's detectives learned that McDonald had been collecting Social Security disability payments that totaled over $20,000. Without a murder warrant, however, Social Security officials would not be able to tell authorities where the checks were being deposited.

After collecting new evidence and presenting it to the District Attorney's Office, a warrant was issued for McDonald charging him with Pang's murder. Now, armed with an arrest warrant, detectives were able to finally obtain the information they needed to capture McDonald.

From that information it appeared that McDonald had returned to Southern California. His disability checks were being deposited into a San Fernando Valley area bank, where a review of bank surveillance camera film showed a woman withdrawing $1,500 from McDonald's account.

Sheriff's detectives would learn that the woman lived on a quiet, tree-lined street in the nearby Reseda neighborhood of Los Angeles. They went to her home hoping to find McDonald. When detectives arrived, the woman fought with them. She was detained while authorities continued their search. McDonald was found hiding inside the home and was finally arrested

Arresting officers were surprised by McDonald's appearance. The conservative, buttoned-down corporate attorney was now a fugitive. McDonald had lost weight and appeared gaunt. He also had shaved his head to alter his appearance.

McDonald's female companion was arrested for harboring a fugitive. She had befriended McDonald in 1997, when both were staying at a Los Angeles area motel. She described his plunge into depression and how he "thought the world was against him." She said McDonald also told her that he was being framed by authorities for a murder he didn't commit.

Prosecutors were now faced with taking McDonald to trial. With only eyewitness testimony and circumstantial evidence, prosecutors would face an uphill battle.

Four years had passed since the murder occurred and prosecutors still had no motive. They could not prove that McDonald or Janie Pang actually knew each other. But, if they could tie the circumstantial evidence together and eliminate other suspects, they could use it to point toward McDonald in an attempt to convince a jury to return a guilty verdict.

That could prove to be difficult, since all McDonald's attorneys needed to do was to refute each piece of evidence and create reasonable doubt in the jury's mind. This would make it more difficult for jurors, under the rule of law and the jury instructions, to return a guilty verdict.

With the case about ready to go to trial, I knew that one of the central pieces of the evidence that would be in dispute was my sketch.

The prosecutor assigned to the case was a highly competent deputy district attorney. He was both intelligent and thoughtful. The prosecutor was also very deliberate. He was a quick study, too, and we met so I could explain the process of how the sketch was developed and why, in my opinion, it resembled McDonald.

When the trial began, the prosecution did not offer

a motive for the killing. They began building the case on evidence that Danny Pang owed McDonald's law firm $20,000 and that McDonald, who was severely in debt, went to the house armed with a handgun to collect the money.

The prosecutor described McDonald as a "manipulative man" who abandoned his family and staged his own death by suicide in an effort to elude authorities and avoid arrest, so he could relocate and begin a new life.

My sketch became an important piece of evidence because the Pangs' housekeeper could not positively identify the gunman. And the neighbor who provided the information for the sketch was reluctant to identify anyone. This left it to me to explain the obvious and subtle similarities between the sketch and a photograph of McDonald taken around the time of the murder.

In my testimony, I talked about the many similarities to the sketch in the shape of McDonald's face, ears and mouth. I also believed that the eyes also bore a resemblance. My opinion that the sketch strongly resembled McDonald was reinforced by the distinctive hairstyle that added to the overall similarity.

McDonald was represented by a highly skilled and competent private trial attorney who was passionate and relentless in his defense. As a police officer, you want to hate guys like him. But if I were in McDonald's shoes, he would be the attorney I would hire to fight for my freedom.

The defense hammered away at the prosecution's case by offering a different explanation for the chain of events. The lawyer told the jury that McDonald was trapped in a "loveless" marriage and that he turned to the company of prostitutes for his emotional fulfillment. McDonald testified that at the time of the murder, he had been in a hotel with a $400 prostitute. Prosecutors were dubious about his account, especially, when they couldn't locate the woman to corroborate the story.

McDonald further testified that he actually intended to commit suicide but, at the last minute, changed his mind. He said that he disappeared to avoid his marriage and a lifestyle he despised. He told the jury that he was unable to provide the wealthy "Newport Beach" lifestyle his wife wanted.

McDonald told the jury that he was far from being the successful attorney that many described. He had racked up $60,000 dollars in credit card debt while trying to provide a lavish lifestyle and yet he still owed money for his daughter's school tuition.

On cross examination, the prosecution countered that McDonald's mounting debt was a strong motive for robbery and that his fleeing the area showed a consciousness of guilt.

McDonald's attorney was unfazed by the prosecution's theories. He continued to hammer away at their case as he raised several issues including: Danny Pang's alleged ties to a Taiwanese organized crime ring, his alleged million-dollar gambling habit and allegations that the victim was planning to divorce him because of domestic violence.

Prosecutors countered that there was never any evidence of organized crime links to Danny Pang or any evidence linking him to her murder.

They also defended the Sheriff's Department investigators from an attack on their competency launched by McDonald's attorney. This criticism stemmed from a late report filed by a detective. The defense attorney alleged that sheriff's detectives failed to interview the last person who spoke to Pang. He also questioned their inability to identify a fingerprint left on the stairs or to find any other evidence that placed McDonald inside Pang's home.

McDonald's attorney also proposed an alternative killer, a man Pang and her husband knew had stalked her since her days as an exotic dancer. The man in question allegedly resembled the sketch, too, but sheriff's detectives were able to eliminate him as a suspect when they verified that he was out of the country at the time of the slaying.

Now, it was my turn to testify. But, when it came time for the defense to cross-examine me, it seemed that the attorney put me on trial instead of simply questioning he sketch.

McDonald's attorney focused on the fact there was no written police report accompanying the sketch. He accused me of being derelict in my duty because he alleged that proper police procedure called for a written report to be completed for each step of an investigation.

The fact was, I was not required to file a written report because the sketch itself was the result of my interview with the eyewitness. Her words formed the basis for the suspect illustrated in the sketch.

Although the attorney was wrong, it didn't matter. All he needed to do was plant the seed of doubt in the jury's mind by making me look incompetent.

In retrospect, I should feel pretty good about the result of the sketch. Although the defense touched on the sketch, he didn't dwell on it and chose instead to make me the issue.

That was fine with me because I had an excellent reputation for honesty and conducting thorough, complete investigations. He chose to misrepresent the facts because the rules of law allowed him to. I guess I could have taken it personally, but it was nothing more than a trial tactic that in the long run, had no effect on my career as a police sketch artist or police officer.

But he was good at his job and was able to get the jury to deadlock ten votes to two for McDonald's acquittal. McDonald walked out of court that day a free man.

Several years later, on Sept. 12, 2009, Danny Pang was found dead near his Newport Beach home. Toxicology reports revealed a lethal dose of oxycodone and hydrocodone in his blood and dozens of undigested pills in his stomach. His death was later ruled to be a suicide.

With McDonald's acquittal and Danny Pang's untimely death, I guess justice for Janie Pang will just have to wait.

MICHAEL W. STREED

Chapter 12
'Our Little Girl …'

"Attention all units and stations, for Station 18, a 207 from the Stanton area … the child is described as a female, white, five years old…"

The crime broadcast at approximately 5:30 p.m. on July 15, 2002, sent chills down my spine. The Orange County Sheriff's Department had initiated a countywide emergency police radio broadcast about a child who had been kidnapped from one of the areas where they provided police services.

After already spending many years in law enforcement, I was conditioned to focus only on "select" countywide emergency broadcasts. Those I paid the most attention to were those crimes occurring closest to my city. The others were nothing more than white noise.

But cases where a child's been stolen by a stranger? That's a whole different ballgame. Before the last word in the broadcast is spoken an adrenaline surge kicks in, and suddenly you're running on all cylinders. In that instance, your total focus is on each word the dispatcher is speaking.

On the evening of the reported child abduction, I was working a uniformed patrol shift for the Orange Police Department. I was assigned to train a recent academy graduate, a police trainee. I remember feeling helpless as he chauffeured us around the city, listening to the emergency radio broadcast that was repeated several times over the next couple of hours. You could tell even the dispatchers were feeling the pressure, as the urgency in the sound of their voice grew with each new broadcast.

At the time of the kidnapping, I had worked closely with many Orange County Sheriff's Department detectives. As both a law enforcement professional and police sketch artist, I enjoyed assisting them with several sexual assault and homicide cases. But I sensed that this case would be different than the rest, so I commented to my partner that we should probably catch up on our work at headquarters, as they would soon be calling and I would have to leave.

I was confident that, if detectives had a good witness, they would call and ask me to assist with a composite sketch. Again, based upon the circumstances and gravity of the case, I knew that it was just a matter of time. The case dynamics would demand my full attention for sure because, from what the broadcast said, this was a stranger kidnapping of a child. In my experience as a parent and as a law enforcement professional, this is THE worst kind of crime imaginable. So I waited, but the call never came.

Halfway into our shift, the emergency broadcasts began to taper off. So, to take my mind off of what happened, I distracted myself by becoming immersed in my own activity. Yet despite how many radio calls we handled throughout the night, the little girl who would soon become known to the world as "Samantha" occupied my thoughts throughout the remainder of my shift.

The pressure I began to feel was tremendous. I had no doubt that I was up for the task because I had been in such situations before. It's just a lot to think about when you know that the case hinges on your sketch.

Earlier in my career, I'd experienced two other high-profile stranger abduction cases involving child victims. Both cases relied heavily on composite sketches at the outset, and the facts of each case presented unique challenges.

The first incident occurred in 1983, when I was asked to assist the San Bernardino County Sheriff's Department in their search for Laura Bradbury, a three-year-old girl from Huntington Beach. Laura had been camping with her family at the Joshua Tree National Park. She disappeared after going to a bathroom with her eight-year-old brother and was reported missing by her family.

During their investigation, sheriff's detectives developed a witness who reported seeing Laura with an unknown adult male. Later, this witness described to me a bearded, scraggly stranger. The resulting sketch provided detectives with their first real clue to what might have happened to Laura.

Unfortunately, the sketch didn't lead to any suspects. What followed, though, was an intensive and exhaustive investigation. It wasn't until years later that authorities found what they believed to be evidence of human body parts that they believed belonged to Laura.

At this writing, no suspects have been located and no arrests made.

My other stranger-abduction case experience came in 1997 with the kidnapping and murder of ten-year-old Anthony Martinez, a case that I detailed in a previous chapter.

Both of these cases were difficult because the witnesses were severely traumatized or didn't see anything. Stranger abduction cases always demand quick action because time can become your worst enemy. The Orange County Sheriff's Department was already on the right track when they immediately broadcast valuable information to law enforcement about Samantha's abduction.

In any criminal investigation, especially cases like these, a good witness is golden. One can often make a difference in bringing the kidnapped child back safe, or if the unthinkable happens, helping bring the suspect to justice.

In rare instances, the opposite occurs. A witness sees the child with their abductor, but they don't realize what they are seeing and cannot provide a useful description to police. Rare is the witness who copies a license plate number or provides a decent vehicle description.

Or, if you have multiple witnesses, all you are likely to get is a variety of descriptions, few of which lead you to believe they saw the same person. The time it takes to pull the information together to determine the most viable witness is valuable time lost.

Again, when it comes to stranger abduction cases – every desperate moment counts! Thankfully, in the Runnion case, they had a witness.

I finally got the call for assistance around midnight from a very tired sheriff's detective. I couldn't help thinking about how much time had already passed. I wished I could have gotten the call and responded earlier. I wondered if my witness could still provide a useful description. But, I couldn't be too critical. Nobody is really prepared for these kinds of cases. They write manuals and develop protocols, but until it happens, no one knows how their agency will react. In Orange County, cases where children are snatched off the street thankfully are rare.

But, when they do happen, the investigation takes on a dynamic that can be chaotic and test an agency's organization skills and their relationship with the community.

One thing the Orange County Sheriff's Department did extremely well during this initial phase of the investigation was to keep everyone organized, informed and moving in the same direction. Most importantly, they never lost sight of the goal of bringing Samantha home safely.

After receiving a quick case overview, I gathered my

sketching materials and took off to meet the detectives, and their eyewitness, at their offices in Stanton.

Before leaving, I took a moment to consider which route I would take to get there. My first thought was to take the freeway, which at that time of night, would be the fastest route. But I had a lot going on in my personal life, and I needed time to think. I also knew how serious this case had become, which made it even more critical that I take time to refocus. With that in mind, I decided that the most direct route via surface streets would be the best for me.

The Orange Police Department, where I worked at the time, was about a block south of Katella Avenue, a major thoroughfare that cut through the heart of Orange County. Coincidentally, the sheriff's office in Stanton was also located off Katella Avenue. For me, it would be a straight shot: no turns, time to think.

As I began my drive through the quiet evening, dark images began filling my head as I slowly passed by the Honda Center and Anaheim Stadium. These cases rarely ended well, and I knew that this case might be one of them. Most of my concern stemmed from the fact that the only evidence they had at the time was the eyewitness description. To provide sheriff's detectives with something useful required that I get it right.

Not far down the road, my mood began to brighten when I suddenly found myself awash in the glow of neon lights as I drove past the Disneyland Resort.

Who wouldn't be happy driving past Disneyland? Doesn't every NFL hero who wins a championship declare that is the first place they are headed while hoisting the Lombardi trophy over their head? Thinking about that image helped lull me from my dark mood. I began to think about going there as a child and how my wife and I took our children there. Those were enjoyable days of fun and laughter. It became a joyful interruption from the rigors of everyday life.

These days, the rigors of everyday life for me meant trying to keep my family together.

The month before, my wife had been diagnosed with breast cancer right after our oldest son left to serve in the Army and face combat. At the same time, our youngest son was graduating high school with a promising life ahead, yet feeling unsure of the fate that awaited the rest of his family.

Forcing myself to re-focus my attention on Samantha's plight snapped me back into reality. Now, all I could think about was where she might be and what kind of sick bastard could pull off such a cowardly act.

When I arrived at the sheriff's station in Stanton, the first thought I had was how eerily quiet it was. If you didn't know the station was there, you would have driven right past it. The building sat back on a small side street off Katella Avenue and was not well lit.

The few cars that drove by from time to time hadn't a clue to the chaos going on inside. It all looked surreal to me. To the casual observer it was a city sleeping peacefully, an image that belied the well-organized manhunt that had already taken shape.

Detectives directed me to park in a secure area, normally reserved for their own deputies, and they ushered me into the station.

Exhausted and grim-looking investigators nodded a quick greeting as they went about their individual assignments. They were determined to find Samantha and worked through their exhaustion single-mindedly focused on bringing her home safely.

Before I met my witness, a detective first briefed me about what they knew so far:

Earlier in the evening, an unidentified man had

approached Samantha and a six-year-old friend, Sarah Ahn, while they played a board game outside the home Samantha shared with her mother, Erin Runnion. He walked toward the girls, asking them for help finding his dog.

As he came closer, he suddenly reached out and grabbed Samantha. The suspect turned, with Samantha in his arms, and ran toward a light green Honda sedan parked nearby.

Bravely trying to fight her way loose, Samantha did everything her mother had taught her to do. Determined to escape, she kicked and fought the whole way to the car, screaming to her friend, "Help me! Go tell my grandma!" The grandmother was baby-sitting Samantha while her mother was at work.

Frightened, Sarah ran home to tell her mother as the man put Samantha into his car and drove off, eluding the first responding units. Sarah would later describe the man to deputies as Hispanic, between the ages of twenty-five and forty, with brown shoulder-length hair, a thin moustache, wearing a button-up, powder-blue shirt.

After being briefed on the case, I met Sarah in a nearby interview room. Over the next couple of hours, she was able to pull the face of Samantha's abductor from her memory and describe him to me. I found the six-year-old witness to be intelligent and courageous. The resulting sketch was given to investigators and was soon viewed worldwide as the search for Samantha expanded.

That summer, it seemed as if child kidnappings were everywhere. It seemed there wasn't a day that went by without the report of another stranger abduction happening somewhere in America.

The FBI tried to downplay the apparent trend saying that in the previous year, 2001, there had been ninety-three stranger abduction cases opened nationwide by the bureau, down from 2000, when the bureau investigated 134.

The National Center for Missing & Exploited Children also weighed in on the subject and commented that while stranger abductions were a "terrible problem" the actual number of cases reported was decreasing. On average, the center said, there are approximately 100 cases reported yearly, down from the approximately 200 to 300 cases a year reported in the early 1980s.

Since being established by Congress in 1984, the National Center for Missing & Exploited Children was becoming a valuable resource for law enforcement. John Walsh, the former host of the popular Fox television show "America's Most Wanted," helped found the center with his wife, Reve. They had begun campaigning for such an organization after their six-year-old son, Adam, was abducted and murdered in 1981.

Since the center opened, it has become the preeminent authority and information clearinghouse for all missing-child cases reported to law enforcement. It also has tried to help the media keep these cases in perspective. Although the media can be an important ally in abduction cases, the manner in which they report the news can sometimes create a distorted view, so the center tries to prevent misinformation regarding a problem like child abduction that could create national hysteria.

After Samantha was abducted, the media was more than willing to help. They did a tremendous job by flooding the airwaves with the sketch of the kidnapper. Everywhere you turned, it was in the newspaper, on the Internet, on television and any pane of window glass where there was room to hang a flyer.

In the first few hours, investigators also notified the U.S. Border Patrol in the event the kidnapper tried to leave the country with Samantha and enter Mexico.

It was also important for detectives to locate Samantha's

biological father, who lived across the country. It is standard practice to notify both parents in abduction cases and to eliminate anyone as a suspect who might remotely be involved.

Derek Jackson, Samantha's father, was located at his home in Massachusetts. Devastated by news of his daughter's abduction, he pleaded desperately in the media for parents to "watch their children closely."

With no known suspects, only the face of the nameless kidnapper, a reward was announced and tips soon began pouring in.

Hoping that a large amount of money would motivate someone to turn in the suspect, British Petroleum, Erin Runnion's employer, had ponied up $50,000. An additional $10,000 came from the Coalition of Police and Sheriffs, a local community law enforcement charity. With $60,000 on the table, detectives figured someone would trip over themselves to get to the phone, provide the suspect's name and cash in.

I think that's the part of rewards that has always bothered me. We have to pay people to do the right thing. But, I learned quickly in my law enforcement career that altruism went out the window long ago!

Erin Runnion contributed human capital by making a tearful plea before the media saying that her daughter was a sweet child and imploring her kidnapper to let her go. She added the family didn't want vengeance, she just wanted her baby back. "Please … just let her go," she said as she ended her statement.

Three days after the abduction, an emergency 911 call came in to the Riverside County Sheriff's Department at approximately 3:17 p.m. The caller, a young man named Justin, was hysterical.

He told the dispatcher, "Oh my God, I found a dead body.

Please hurry, ok? I'm in the Ortegas, OK? Ortega Mountains. I'm in Riverside County, OK? Listen to me, I'm scared to sit here, there's another truck up the street, and we want to get out of here, we're scared."

The dispatcher spoke to him and kept her composure as he went on to say, "It's a baby. I think it may even be that little girl that's been on the news. It's a little girl. I swear. We looked and as soon as we seen, I left. I don't know what to do."

Too frightened to stay with the body because he feared the killer might be lurking nearby, he met deputies at his house. He led them back to Killen Trail, off the Ortega Highway, an area popular with locals and hang glider enthusiasts near Lake Elsinore.

It was there they found the nude body of a little girl, matching Samantha's physical description. The killer hadn't made any efforts to hide her body. He left it out in the open in what was perceived to be a taunting challenge to authorities.

It wasn't long though before everyone's worst fears were realized – the body was positively identified as Samantha's.

Crime scene investigators collected evidence from the scene, and an autopsy found that Samantha had been sexually assaulted and asphyxiated. Authorities theorized that her attacker had kept her alive for several hours before killing her.

As the case gained momentum, law enforcement resources continued to pour in. A cold-blooded murder like this meant that authorities had to catch the suspect quickly before he snatched another child off the street.

Before long, there would be over 400 investigators assigned to the case, 300 sheriff's deputies and a hundred FBI agents, as well as officers from local agencies.

In a show of cooperation, the Riverside County Sheriff's Department allowed the Orange County Sheriff's Department to handle the murder investigation even though Samantha's body had been found in its jurisdiction.

Samantha's brazen abduction and murder drew national attention. President George W. Bush ordered Attorney General John Ashcroft to devote all "necessary federal resources" to the Orange County Sheriff's Department. Even FBI Director Robert Mueller became involved, directing agents to develop a criminal profile of the killer.

Federal agents also deployed Rapid Start, a software system developed to handle the thousands of tips that were pouring in. The system, used in several previous major investigations, helped to organize and collate leads. The system helped determine which leads were more important as well as make sure there was no duplication in the way deputies and agents followed up the leads. Working around the clock, from fifteen to thirty sheriff's deputies and FBI clerks began inputting thousands of leads that investigators would begin chasing all over the country.

This manhunt was of a magnitude rarely seen in Orange County. With all the manpower and resources being thrown into the investigation, it would have been easy for confusion to reign. During my career, I have seen similar investigations reduced to chaos because of internal squabbling between agencies. But that was not the case here.

Mike Carona, the sheriff of Orange County, stepped up and led early on. His inspiring leadership and personal strength surfaced from the outset of the investigation. Combining the sheer force of his personality with single-minded determination, he kept all resources organized and all personnel focused on one thing – bringing Samantha's killer to justice. The second-term sheriff would soon become the main spokesman for the investigation.

Making daily appearances before the news media, he became an image of calm for a public beginning to panic about a killer in their midst. A dedicated family man with his own children, Carona's occasional show of emotion was tempered by steely nerves and firm resolve as he repeatedly challenged the killer over the next few agonizing days.

By now, the reward fund had surged to $100,000. Detectives began checking the files of the several hundred registered sex offenders in and around Orange County, in particular to find whether any of them owned a green car like the one the witness described.

Meanwhile, analysts at the FBI's Behavioral Sciences Unit in Washington, D.C., were reviewing digital crime scene photos of the area where Samantha's body was found. From these photos and other information supplied to them, a behavioral profile of the killer began to develop.

Based on limited information but working from known facts and evidence, the profilers theorized he might kill again. They believed that he was someone who was impulsive and had a short fuse. Their opinion was based on the way he behaved during the kidnapping and undisclosed evidence found around Samantha's body.

They thought that, since the killing, he would have exhibited a radical behavior change and might be missing from work. The profilers theorized that he would have turned to, or stopped, smoking or drinking, or that he might have become more religious. He also would be someone who was unnaturally interested in news reports about Samantha's death.

Since the killer left Samantha's body in the open with a wealth of physical evidence, the profilers thought the killer was taunting the police to try to catch him.

The profilers also believed that the abduction may have started as a sex crime that escalated into a decision to kill the girl. They were also fairly sure the suspect had previously committed sex crimes against children, yet they were unsure if he had killed before.

The profile, coupled with the sketch, would become a powerful tool for detectives.

Criminal profiling was not new to Orange County sheriff's detectives. The discipline had been employed in thousands of cases over the years and continues to be a developing science. In many cases, profiles have been astonishingly accurate and, like composite sketches, helped police eliminate many suspects while allowing them to focus on a narrower pool of candidates.

But, as one longtime FBI profiler commented, profiling can't replace other investigative methods. He described it as being more of a complementary tool. Dr. Park Dietz, a prominent Orange County forensic psychiatrist, further described it as "not just a science – it's a bit of science that requires a great deal of experience and a bit of intuition."

Dietz had worked closely with the FBI over the years, conducting in-depth interviews with John Hinckley Jr., who attempted to assassinate President Ronald Reagan, and Jeffrey Dahmer, a serial killer and cannibal from Milwaukee.

Some were concerned that an incomplete preliminary profile had been released. Their fears were lessened by experts who said that profiles are not necessarily carved in stone and are constantly updated as new and better information becomes available.

In this case, it became important to release the profile as soon as possible in an effort to alert parents to the continuing danger, as the killer had not yet been identified, and to encourage people to call with any information they might have about a possible suspect.

Sheriff Carona continued to update the investigation as he spoke to the entire country and also to the killer. He told the public that the suspect had likely changed his appearance and might have injuries to his hands, arms or face.

Carona also reassured the public that the killer would likely be identified because of the significant amount of forensic evidence that he left behind. He went on to warn that, however, based on that evidence, authorities believed that the killer could strike again soon.

Then, addressing the killer directly, Carona told him that when he took Samantha, he took "our little girl." He gave the killer an ominous warning, "Don't sleep. Don't eat. We are coming after you and will use every resource we have to bring you to justice."

His comments drew national attention and received mixed reviews from experts and media pundits, most of them favorable. He was a sheriff who they said "shot from his heart" and within days became a symbol of strength and hope across the country.

Though criticized by some for his ominous warning about the killer striking again soon, most experts believed that was a carefully scripted statement drafted by the FBI in an effort to make the suspect lay low.

The last thing they wanted was to have him out there stalking young children again before they had an opportunity to analyze evidence and track down more leads. They knew that causing him to feel pressure might cause him to make a mistake. One thing they knew from previous cases was that if this suspect was a serial killer, he would refine his technique as time wore on, making him more difficult to capture.

To further support the investigation and provide extra incentive for tips on the killer, more reward money was added by California Gov. Gray Davis. This brought the total reward fund to $150,000 as more leads continued to pour in.

Finally, they got the lead they were waiting for.

Someone called with a name of a person they believed strongly resembled my sketch: Alejandro Avila, a twenty-seven-year-old Hispanic man. It turned out that Avila lived in Lake Elsinore near where Samantha's body was found.

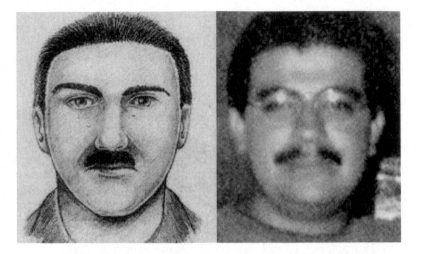

Author's sketch is on the left, Avila's photo is on the right.

Detectives soon located and detained Avila, spending the next several hours interviewing him as other detectives executed search warrants at the homes of his family members.

Avila denied his involvement, offering an alibi. He told detectives that he was at a shopping mall, in another county, near the Ontario International Airport at the time of the kidnapping.

Detectives arrested him anyway and began examining his alibi. They located cellphone and credit card records that instead placed Avila in the southern Orange County area at the time of Samantha's abduction.

This was significant because although Stanton is in western Orange County, several miles from southern Orange County, the Ortega Highway begins in southern Orange County and cuts through the hills into Riverside County. The highway, an area that's seen its share of murders and body dumps over the years, ends just south of Lake Elsinore, near where the body was found and where Avila lived with his mother.

Sheriff Carona would soon announce Avila's arrest and declare that they were "100 percent" sure they had the person responsible for Samantha's murder. The nation breathed a collective sigh of relief when President Bush himself declared Avila's presumptive guilt.

The District Attorney's Office quickly filed charges against Avila for murder occurring during a kidnapping and sexual assault, charges supported by evidence collected during the investigation that had not been released to the public. Local media reported unnamed sources confirming there was a DNA match between Avila and evidence collected from the area where Samantha's body was found.

If he were found guilty on those charges, Avila could face the death penalty.

Controversy soon began to swirl around the case as critics decried declarations in the media of Avila's presumptive guilt made by public officials.

The public was also angry by reports that a jury, only a year earlier, had acquitted Avila of charges he molested an ex-girlfriend's two daughters. In that case, a Riverside County jury rejected the allegations against Avila despite compelling testimony and reports of threats Avila allegedly made against the girls' family.

Other allegations soon surfaced against Avila of sexual harassment at his former place of employment.

All of this was occurring while District Attorney Tony Rackauckas, who was mentioned in an earlier chapter, mulled whether he should seek the death penalty against Avila.

After conferring with other deputies in his office and with Samantha's mother, Rackauckas decided to file a special circumstances allegation against Avila qualifying him for the death penalty. Under California law, if a jury were to find Avila guilty and agree that Samantha's death occurred in the course of her abduction and sexual assault then that same jury could vote he be put to death during the penalty phase of the trial.

Afterward Rackauckas declared, "Anyone who commits an act like this in Orange County will either die in prison of natural causes or will be executed."

He added, "This type of crime is extraordinary. It's extraordinarily destructive ... not only because of the violence it brings on a single family but because of the suffering and fear it brings on an entire community, in this case, the entire nation."

Ironically, it was reported that before Avila's arrest, while he and his mother watched news accounts of the murder, she suggested that whoever did it should be "tied up and burned alive" -- while Avila himself suggested "the electric chair" for the killer.

Justice for Samantha would take time. After much legal wrangling by his defense attorneys, Avila's trial was scheduled to begin in January 2004. Three years later, the case came to a close when Avila was convicted of Samantha's murder and was sentenced to death.

Many of us have been inextricably tied to Samantha through our involvement in the case. I know that upon Avila's arrest, I was flooded with media interview requests and tried to grant all of them. I wanted the public to know how important a police sketch artist can be to a case by telling them how important witnesses are, even witnesses who are children.

People remark to me all the time about Sarah Ahn, "She was only six years old! How was she able to describe him?" My answer to them is simple: She was able to remain calm and was extremely intelligent. Her willingness to assist and the fact that she realized the enormity of the situation showed great maturity for someone of such a young age.

Sadly, there will be more Samanthas. But I believe that

with strong, courageous leaders who support strengthening our laws to protect children and support law enforcement's use of innovative technologies, we can make a difference.

Many of us who were involved in the case were changed forever. After the case, I became known as the artist who sketched Samantha's killer. Every time I was introduced, this case was mentioned. It's as if I had never sketched any other case, or had any other successes, because this one meant so much. But there were many other people who contributed to the success of the investigation, too. It's almost embarrassing to receive so many accolades.

In my eyes, Sarah and Samantha are the real heroes. Without Sarah's description and her willingness to work with me, there was no way Avila would have been identified. It's brave people like her that make my job that much easier. And I think Samantha's determination to survive that night helped cause Avila to make mistakes and become careless enough to leave a trove of evidence behind that helped lead to his conviction.

Who could ask for better role models?

Chapter 13
Gotcha

Police work, though fraught with danger, can be a challenging and rewarding career. For all its physical demands, there's a mental aspect to the job that can be exhausting too. But I wouldn't have it any other way. I loved being a cop and reveled in spending over thirty years working in the world's largest open-air playground.

As police officers, we work tirelessly in our communities to keep them safe. Each of us came into the job for a variety of reasons, but most of all it was because we wanted to make a difference.

I was one of those who not only wanted to make a difference, but also sought to be different. That is why I became The SketchCop. I wanted to extend my reach by having an additional tool to identify and help arrest the "bad guys."

When I was a police officer, it was easy to see whether I was making a difference. Arrest statistics became the numbers game that management used to gauge our effectiveness.

But for police sketch artists, the effectiveness might take months or even years to measure. Until there's an arrest and booking photo to compare to the sketch, we just have to keep working with the faith that the sketch we provide will at some point make a difference in a case. Cases that linger on are the most frustrating for me because there is a victim left hanging in the balance waiting for justice.

Thankfully, there are some dumb crooks out there who unselfishly relieve victims and eyewitnesses of the burden of aiding an investigation while feeding our curiosity as police sketch artists. I say "dumb crook" in jest, because I'm sure it's not their intent to get caught. But regardless of how they are discovered, it's all good by me.

Opposite the careless crooks are the successful ones. They prove to be the most challenging variety. Oftentimes they are professional, career criminals who will go to great lengths to prepare and plan their crimes, making sure no one sees their face. They also avoid leaving any trace of identification along the way.

But sometimes they, too, get caught. In my experience, they get caught in the same way that people become random victims of crime: from poor timing, bad luck and placing themselves in a position of jeopardy. All of these reasons are contributing factors.

I've got to smile when a "dumb crook" drops his wallet containing identification at a crime scene or when bank robbers make the not-unfamiliar mistake of staring into the surveillance camera while spraying paint on the lens, trying to hide their participation in the crime after we've already gotten a perfect look at their face.

Sometimes you've got to wonder why criminals take such risks in the first place. In my experience, crimes are committed for three basic reasons: need, desire and opportunity.

Each of the cases I will discuss now are examples of those three reasons. Some of them stand alone as an example, while some cases include a combination of the three.

The first, need, can be a powerful motivator. Most people

need something. Honest people work for what they need. However, crooks who need drugs, alcohol, food or money often just go out and take it, even if they hurt a few people along the way.

A crook not motivated to work for what he needs will rarely go far from home to commit crimes, mostly because they lack reliable transportation and are familiar with the surrounding area. Some are just plain lazy!

For them, small neighborhood businesses become attractive targets. The criminal's predatory nature and profiling skills make places of business with unskilled labor and poor security systems especially vulnerable. The criminal views them as being easy to pick off and a source of quick, easy cash.

I recall one such business in Orange. It was a burger joint located on a major street straddling a commercial and residential area with nearby bus stops. The area was vibrant and bustled with heavy foot traffic from employees of nearby industrial businesses, drawn by the smell of fresh, charbroiled burgers wafting through the air. The place was always busy and from personal experience I can tell you why. Their food was good!

On March 28, 1996, at approximately 7:30 p.m., a Hispanic man entered the business through the open front door and began speaking Spanish to a cook and a waitress who were seated in a booth near the front door, taking a break. He asked if he could use the bathroom, so they directed him there and continued talking. They had no idea that the suspect was a wanted felon who recently went AWOL from his parole officer.

The suspect, who would later be identified as Richard Garcia, age twenty-eight, disappeared into the bathroom and when he came out walked directly back to the employees. As he approached the woman, he reached under his shirt, pulling out a chrome-plated .25 caliber, semi-automatic handgun.

He pointed the gun at her and he shouted at her, "Give me all your money!" Panicked and unable to move, she froze as her male co-worker began to get up from the table. Garcia reacted quickly by placing the barrel of his gun against the man's ribcage and firing a single round into him at point blank range.

As the man fell backward onto the table, Garcia pointed the gun back at the woman as he again demanded, "Get up and give me all your money. Now!" This time she moved behind the counter and emptied the contents of the cash register, which amounted to about $350.

The gunman remained calm and restrained the wounded man with a hand on his shoulder while he kept his gun pointed at the woman and told her to put the money on the counter. After taking the money, he left the restaurant and ran down the main thoroughfare toward a residential area.

When the waitress was sure the gunman was gone, she called 911. Paramedics transported the man to a local trauma center where surgeons performed life-saving surgery. As one of the police officers on the scene, I was directed to follow the victim to the hospital to collect any evidence.

At the hospital, a technician handed me the man's clothing so I could book them for later examination by forensic technicians. As I was folding his shirt, a bullet fell out onto the floor. Initially it had appeared as if the victim had suffered two gunshot wounds, but apparently the bullet had gone through him and gotten caught up in his clothing. In their haste to save his life, detectives and paramedics hadn't looked inside the shirt he wore.

When I returned to the station to book the evidence, detectives asked me to interview the female witness for the purpose of developing a sketch of the suspect. Ideally, I would have spoken to the shooting victim, but he was delirious from the pain of his gunshot wound and unable to speak. So, I was left with the shaken waitress to interview.

The situation was made slightly more complicated because she didn't speak English. But a Spanish language translator, who was also a police officer, helped me communicate with her. Now, all I had to do was calm her. Even though a couple of hours had passed, she was still highly traumatized after seeing her friend shot and gravely wounded.

It was important that we try to obtain a sketch as soon as practical, so I began to interview her carefully. She proved to be a good witness. The waitress was able to help me construct an image of a man who wore a baseball cap and had a distinctive mole on his right cheek. His eyes stared out from the sketch with a "dead" expression. At the conclusion of the interview, she was pleased with the image and I congratulated her for the courage she displayed at the restaurant and for taking an active role in the investigation.

Author's sketch is on the left, Garcia's photo is on the right.

Detectives took the sketch to the hospital the following day and showed it to the shooting victim. He was pleased with how the sketch turned out. He remembered the mole and added that the suspect had some chin hair and appeared to be growing a goatee. Even more important than the description was that he told detectives the suspect was a man who had come into the restaurant a couple of months before with a female companion, who filled out a job application. Others at the restaurant also remembered the suspect coming there several times over the previous months to eat, sometimes accompanied by children.

Detectives raced over to the restaurant and began examining job applications and quickly found the one they were searching for. The woman, in her identifying information, listed a residence only a few blocks from the restaurant. The short distance meant that a suspect could have gotten there quickly, especially after shooting someone and fleeing from the police.

Within an hour, three detectives knocked on the door to the apartment, which was answered by the female job applicant. Invited inside, they told her they suspected Garcia was hiding there. She looked toward the bedroom and indicated he was in the shower. She added that he was armed and that had told her he would not go back to prison.

Detectives carefully and quietly entered the bedroom and saw a nearby closet. They called out to the suspect, who answered that he was armed and would not come out. For the next few moments, detectives engaged in tense negotiations to broker his surrender.

Garcia first opened the door slightly and tossed his gun out before surrendering himself. As detectives took him into custody they saw that a mole just below his right eye, just as described by the witness.

After Garcia's arrest, detectives interviewed his

associates, who confirmed having earlier conversations with him in which he described his desire to rob the restaurant because he said, "It would be easy." He added that he and the woman needed money for the kids to buy food.

As a matter of fact, while the shooting victim was at the hospital, fighting for his life, Garcia and the woman and kids were feasting on fast food purchased with money from the holdup.

Garcia later admitted to shooting the victim but blamed it on the man for "trying to play Superman."

His parole officer described Garcia best in his follow-up report when he wrote, "Clearly, parolee's current charges appear extremely callous, with strong disregard for a lawful existence."

The judge apparently agreed and sentenced Garcia to ninety-three years to life in prison.

The second type of criminal is one who is motivated by desire. He may not necessarily need what he is looking for, but he takes it anyway. His desire can be so strong that his crimes become predatory in nature. Sex crimes fit within this particular motivation.

And while other criminal types stay close to home, the predator is more cunning. He carefully plans his crimes and has a preferred victim profile. Oftentimes he will wander far from home to avoid being recognized while seeking his prey.

Serial rapist Steven Morales fit that pattern. A married father of two young children, he supported his family by working in construction. He lived outside of Orange County in Chino Hills, California, and began targeting young women during late August 1998 through early January 1999.

After his crime spree began, detectives in four Orange County cities began to notice similarities in cases. Using a sophisticated computer software program managed by the Orange County District Attorney's Office, detectives were able to tie several crimes together by the suspect description, victim profile and ultimately the matching of biological evidence through DNA testing.

Morales surfaced for the first time in the city of Tustin in August 1998. His victim, a sixteen-year-old high school student, was walking in a residential area when approached by Morales. He was cruising along in a distinctive looking blue Chevrolet pickup truck with custom body parts. He stopped and asked her about the location of a particular high school. When she stopped to answer him, he pointed a gun at her and said, "Get in or I'll kill you. Don't cry or scream."

He drove the girl to a commercial area, where he sexually assaulted her. He told her that members of the 18th Street gang, a notoriously violent Los Angeles street gang, were watching the assault. Morales told the victim that he had kidnapped and raped her to get into the gang. He further threatened to hurt her if she reported it, then he blindfolded her and drove a short distance before abandoning her on a street.

I met with her at the Tustin Police Department to conduct a composite sketch interview. She was a diminutive young lady who remained very quiet.

During the interview she was calm and seemed detached. Some might mistake that for indifference, a symptom of a time when teens are so overexposed to violence that they just don't care. I didn't think that at all. I recognized that her behavior was the numbness associated with a highly traumatic incident. In the end, I was able to get through to her, and she provided a very detailed description, right down to describing the man's crooked yellow teeth.

Author's sketch is on the left, Morales' photo is on the right.

In October 1998 Morales reappeared in Huntington Beach. His next victims were two sisters, ages thirteen and sixteen. They had been hanging out, smoking cigarettes, when Morales approached them and identified himself as a police officer. He didn't display any identification, yet they still accompanied him to a nearby vacant office building where he sexually assaulted them. As in the previous case, he threatened to "come back and get them" if they reported what happened.

Morales' attacks continued into November that year as he shifted his method of attack. This time he broke into the Seal Beach residence of a forty-six-year-old woman. He waited for his victim to return, concealing himself behind a bedroom door, and confronted her with a knife taken from her kitchen.

Morales told her, "I'm not going to hurt you if you do what I say." He tied her up with a bootlace and tried to sexually assault her, but he couldn't complete the act. He referred to her as "lady" and blamed her for making him nervous and unable to finish his assault. Morales asked for money and passed up expensive jewelry in favor of her purse, which he stole from her car.

Later, while police were inside her home taking the report, Morales called her phone twice. He taunted the police investigator who answered and told him to tell the victim that he had a nice view into her bedroom. Police traced the call to a phone booth in Buena Park, but they were unable to catch him. Witnesses described a vehicle leaving the area that matched the suspect's vehicle from previous assaults.

Morales' last known attack occurred in Irvine in early January 1999. Like the Seal Beach attack, this was also a "hide in" burglary. Once again, Morales hid behind a bedroom door and surprised his victim, a seventeen-year-old high school student. He was not armed but was able to wrestle the victim onto her bed where he covered her face and bound her hands and feet.

Morales told her, "Don't try anything, don't fuck with me. I just want some money." He proceeded to sexually assault her and threatened to take photos of her and post them online if she reported the crime.

Detectives on the cases got to work trying to tie them together, examining any piece of evidence that might help identify the attacker. Although my sketch from the Tustin case had been published in the newspaper, it was only released locally and didn't make it to adjoining counties that surrounded Orange County.

It had been approximately four months since the suspect's last sexual assault, but detectives noted that he was escalating his behavior as he became bolder with each new attack, using fear and intimidation to control his victims. He was also refining his methods, frustrating detectives who feared he would soon strike again.

Detective Darrell Hardin of the Seal Beach Police Department was assigned to investigate the sexual assault in his city. Hardin was an experienced detective who was smart enough to realize what this crime meant to the small beachside hamlet whose economy depended heavily on tourist trade and parking citation revenue.

That gave Hardin an idea. It was unlikely that the suspect would have parked right in front of his victim's residence. He would most likely have parked a short distance away and walked there. The assault occurred on a day when street sweepers traversed the city scrubbing the streets clean, so there was a parking moratorium in residential areas and offending vehicles were mercilessly cited.

Hardin began reviewing all parking citations issued in a perimeter around the victim's Seal Beach residence on the day of the assault. After sifting through a stack of parking citations, he struck pay dirt. A vehicle matching the description of the one used in previous assaults had been issued a street sweeping citation two blocks from the victim's residence.

Detectives contacted the owner of the vehicle, Morales, who said he had been in Seal Beach that day to solicit business door-to-door. Police found his story dubious and later obtained his driver's license photo to use in a photographic line-up shown to two of the victims.

They quickly selected Morales' photo as their attacker. Detectives went to Chino Hills with an arrest warrant. After they arrested Morales, they served a search warrant and obtained his DNA sample. They were able to develop a profile that matched DNA left at crime scenes that linked him to the series of sexual assaults. Morales' arrest in July 1999 finally brought an end to the yearlong spree.

When Morales appeared in court to face the judge, he tried

a gambit to get a more lenient sentence. He pleaded guilty, saying he wanted to spare the victims and his family the pain of a trial. He believed his feigned show of compassion would be rewarded with mercy from the court. It didn't work. The judge handed him one of the harshest sentences in recent memory for a serial rapist, 101 years in prison.

Morales will become eligible for parole when he's 118 years old.

The sentencing became a face-off between Morales and the victims. They were supported by friends and family who accompanied them to court. During the proceedings they were able to lash out at Morales and describe the pain he caused them as well as the effect he had on their lives.

In an emotional scene, they cried and shouted at Morales as if they were exorcizing an evil tormenter from their lives. Morales sat and listened impassively showing no emotion.

When it became Morales' turn to address the court he gave no explanation or insight as to why he raped, only commenting, "You may wonder, 'Why you?'"

Morales went on to say that the crimes "were no more planned than wanting my wife, our children, families and friends to feel pain. Explaining this is never going to be easy, and for lack of a better word, unfortunately tragedies similar to this happen to many people all over the world."

I find it pretty outrageous that he would trivialize his actions, reducing them to nothing more than a footnote in a world full of other horrible tragedies. Turning the focus back on Morales, one of the victims' fathers yelled at him, "When you're put in your cell at night … you'll sit and wonder that (your daughter) doesn't run into (someone) like you!"

Sometimes cases are solved through hard work and an active imagination. In the Morales case, that kind of out-of-the-box thinking paid large dividends.

The third and last motivation for committing crimes that

I will discuss is opportunity.

We label people that take advantage of others opportunists. Among criminals, opportunists are always the ones hanging around manipulating others or waiting for the right time to commit their crime.

One of my most successful cases was commissioned by the Long Beach Police Department. I assisted their Sex Crimes Unit with many difficult sexual assault cases for several years. They are an aggressive unit that solves many crimes and yet, for all the evil they see, they are one of the most compassionate groups of detectives I have ever worked with.

On Nov. 29, 1994, a Long Beach family had reported their eight-year-old daughter missing. They told police a family acquaintance had been visiting their home for the day. The drifter, known only as "Kelley," fancied himself a cowboy and favored Western garb. Some called him "Cowboy Kelley."

The man asked the child's father if he could take her to a local carwash. The father wisely declined but later allowed him to walk her to a local market. Once out of sight, Kelley lied to the girl and told her that her father had said she could go with him in his car. When they failed to return, the father telephoned the police.

Detectives began investigating. When questioned about the suspect's real name and identity, no one really knew who he was.

I was called to meet with the father. We worked together for a couple of hours on a composite sketch. He was quite detailed about Kelley's description, but that was no surprise to me because he had spent a considerable amount of time with him. Also, he was traumatized by the loss of his child, but not by having known the man.

To me this meant that his recall and recognition skills

were good. Despite that, it seemed that I had to work hard to get information from him. He just didn't seem as helpful as I thought he could be, or as forthcoming as he should have been. Something was wrong for sure, but I couldn't put my finger on it. The sketch received wide dissemination and would later prove vital in identifying the man.

Author's sketch is on the left, Beckham's photo is on the right.

Later that afternoon, a passer-by saw the girl wandering down a desert road near Moreno Valley. The Riverside County Sheriff's Department took her into protective custody and notified the Long Beach Police Department.

Detective Jana Blair had been assigned the case from the start. I had worked with her on other cases requiring police sketches and found her to be a wonderful person, well-suited for dealing with sensitive cases involving children. Smart and aggressive, she added that feminine, sometimes motherly touch that cases require from time to time.

Blair made the decision to drive out there with her supervisor, then Sgt. Diana Walton. As Sgt. Walton looked on, Blair got down onto the floor to talk to the eight-year-old and play with her at a level where she would not be fearful or intimidated. Her approach worked, and the girl disclosed to Blair that she had been sexually molested by the man known as "Cowboy Kelley."

The victim told Blair that he drove her to remote desert area of Riverside County and that when they stopped he asked if she'd like to play a game.

He told her to take the shoelaces from her shoes, then he proceeded to use them to tie her hands over her head, behind the front passenger seat headrest. After molesting her, he let the girl out of the car and told her that if she repeated some nonsense phrases he created, she would be able to see an Indian Princess. He drove off and left her abandoned by the side of the road without concern for her personal safety.

A couple of months passed as detectives tried to identify their suspect. A break in the case came in January 1995 when the television show "Hard Copy" profiled Kelley Beckham, a modern day "horse rustler," who would go to work on ranches and offer to exercise owners' horses before riding off with them. A "dead-ringer" for my sketch, police soon named Beckham as a suspect in the abduction and molestation investigation.

They learned that, besides being a drifter, Beckham was quite adept at winning people's trust. He like to frequent areas with a heavily gay population. He would hang out at gay bars to meet unwitting targets of his scams. After befriending a man, he would go back to his home that night to sleep, eat his food and later steal his car. Beckham oftentimes got away with it when the men became reluctant to report the thefts for fear of embarrassment.

Police finally found him after he rode a horse up to a bar in Palm Springs and tied the horse up outside, just like in the movies. It wasn't long before a sharp-eyed patron recognized him as a wanted suspect and telephoned police, who took him into custody.

I later spoke to Detective Blair after she interviewed Beckham. She said that he didn't have any previous child molestation history and that it was her opinion that he was acting as an opportunist more than anything else. While it didn't diminish the harm he did to the child by kidnapping and molesting her, it fit the pattern he had long ago established as being an opportunist and taking whatever it was that happened to suit him at the time.

Blair also shared with me the reason the girl's father wasn't all that helpful during the course of the investigation. She had gotten a panicked phone call from the child's mother telling Blair that the father had been arrested for armed robbery. She said he had never gone on television to do interviews and plead for his child's return as he feared he would be recognized by his robbery victims.

The father's crimes qualified him for a "third-strike" felony in California, which translated to a sentence of twenty-five years to life. No wonder I had trouble getting information from him.

As police officers, we always joked about the job security that criminals afforded us. However, as a police sketch artist, I am dead serious about the time and dedication I spend working with victims to take these crooks off the street.

And as long as I can hold onto a pencil, I will always be there.

Chapter 14
The Draw Squad

In every career, there are people widely recognized as leaders in their chosen fields. Police sketch artists are no exception. Many achieve success in high-profile cases and have an uncanny ability to connect with people.

Throughout the course of my career, I have been fortunate enough to be mentored by some of the best. Over the years, I have forged relationships with many of these dedicated people, who have been kind enough to teach me their secrets to success. This meant spending several thousands of miles in the air, hundreds of dollars in telephone bills and several thousand dollars in course tuition fees and related expenses only to learn one thing – there is still much more for me to learn!

In this chapter, I have chosen to profile three police sketch artists who were considered masters in the field. Later, they became friends and colleagues who played an important role in my professional development. All of the men you are about to meet were there for me from the beginning. Their humility and work ethic was displayed through their work. They were strong influences from the beginning, and I am grateful to them for their tutelage.

These men have made history while making other

significant contributions to the field. I like to call them "The Draw Squad."

I hope you enjoy reading their stories as much as I do sharing them with you. Some of the cases you will recognize, while others you might be reading about for the very first time. Either way, the skills they possessed will astound you and the courage of the victims they helped will for sure inspire you.

J. Horace Heafner, FBI and National Center for Missing & Exploited Children

In a career spanning forty-one years with the FBI and later continuing with the National Center for Missing & Exploited Children, J. Horace Heafner provided a strong career influence for many of today's police sketch artists.

An accomplished artist in his own right, Heafner spent many years supervising the FBI's Visual Information Unit as well as training a cadre of police sketch artists as the chief instructor in their composite drawing and photo retouching course. Police sketch artists throughout the world have benefited and thrived under his tutelage. Even many years after he retired, Heafner made frequent appearances an instructor in classes.

A dedicated family man, Heafner, who died in 2014, was also widely known for his work on behalf of missing children.

While working at the National Center for Missing & Exploited Children, he pioneered facial imaging and age-progression techniques that were considered innovative. Through his efforts, police sketch artists have learned to use computer technology to simulate facial aging in photographs of long- missing children.

What I found most impressive, after attending his course, was that Heafner had never used computer graphics software and photo retouching software during his work with the National Center for Missing & Exploited Children, which has since become a leading innovator in the use of facial imaging technology.

Several children were recovered through Heafner's work at the center. Today, the center's staff continues to carry on their groundbreaking work using more modern computer technology.

Heafner hailed from Charlotte, North Carolina, where he attended local public schools. Later, he graduated from the Abbott School of Fine and Commercial Art with an art degree, emphasizing studies in portraiture.

He received an appointment to the FBI in 1945 and worked as a clerk in the fingerprint section before his career was interrupted by military service during the Korean War.

After the war, he returned to the FBI and went to work in the Laboratory Division, researching the application of facial imaging and demonstrative evidence for forensic application during investigations and later in trials conducted in U.S. District Courts.

Over the years, he rose through the ranks of the Laboratory Division and became chief of the Visual Information Unit. During this assignment, he worked on a number of major cases including the assassination of President John F. Kennedy, the Kent State University shootings, Black Panther Party shootings in Chicago, the abduction of newspaper heiress Patty Hearst, the assassination of Dr. Martin Luther King Jr., the murder conviction of Green Beret physician Dr. Jeffrey MacDonald, the Walker family spy case and the attempted assassination of President Ronald Reagan.

His contribution to the King assassination investigation was one of his more notable and historic cases.

Heafner recounted how on April 4, 1968, at about 7:00 p.m., the special agent in charge of the Memphis FBI Office telephoned FBI Director J. Edgar Hoover to report to that King had been shot and killed. An unknown assailant fired on King as he walked onto a balcony of the Lorraine Motel with the Rev. Jesse Jackson and several other friends.

From a block away, the gunman fired the single shot that struck King in the face, the bullet passing through to his spinal cord. He was rushed to the hospital, where he died a short time later. In the pandemonium that followed, a witness saw a white man exiting a nearby rooming house. The witness saw the man leave a rifle wrapped in a sheet in a storefront entrance along with a bag containing binoculars and other personal effects. He walked to the end of the block where he got into a parked white Ford Mustang and drove away.

Two days later, Heafner was told to pack his bags and prepare to take a flight to Birmingham, Alabama. Orders came from FBI Headquarters instructing him to be on an 8:00 p.m. flight from Washington, D.C.

As Heafner prepared for his trip, the nation's capital was gripped by chaos in the streets outside of Justice Department Headquarters, as people began rioting in protest of King's murder. People reacted angrily by breaking windows and setting fires, taunting local police and National Guardsmen. Heafner knew that getting safely out of the building and to the airport would difficult. Luckily, he was able to board the last plane out of Washington, D.C., that evening.

The following day he was instructed to conduct an interview for a suspect sketch with the man who sold a Remington 30.06 Gamemaster 760 rifle, with a Redfield telescopic sight, to someone calling himself "Harvey Lowmeyer."

When it came time during the interview to discuss details of Lowmeyer's face, the man apologized for drawing a "blank." He explained that business had been brisk that afternoon and he was busy selling many guns. He called his memory of the man's facial details "hazy." One detail he did remember: Lowmeyer had "steel blue" eyes.

After completing his interview, Heafner was sent to Memphis. There, he would interview the owner of a pawn shop who sold a pair of binoculars to an unidentified male suspect. The pawn shop owner was able to give some information about the suspect's face that was consistent with information Heafner had previously learned in Birmingham, but once again – no sketch.

Heafner said there was great pressure to come up with a composite sketch and identify the suspect. He had worked at the FBI long enough to know that Director Hoover would personally monitor this case. The special agent in charge would be required to provide Hoover with daily status reports and updates as they occurred.

During Hoover's reign, from the FBI's creation in 1935 until his death in 1976, no one in the bureau wanted to draw *any* negative attention from the director. Thus far, Heafner was getting little information from his eyewitnesses, but he did the best he could, hoping his next witness could expand on information from earlier ones.

Heafner next met with the woman who managed the rooming house from where the fatal shot was fired. Upon arriving, he was met by the manager's "hostile" boyfriend, who threatened to assault him. He mistakenly thought Heafner and the agents with him were some of the reporters who kept bothering them during the investigation. Once he learned they were federal agents, he calmed down and allowed Heafner to conduct his interview. He was allowed into the assassin's room and was able to peer out the bathroom window, through which Heafner shared the same view as the killer. The vantage point allowed him to clearly see the balcony where King had stood before being shot.

Now that he had an idea of what occurred, he was able to interview the hotel manager. She remembered renting the room to the suspect and was able to provide Heafner with vivid facial details. From the descriptions he collected, Heafner was able to produce a composite sketch of King's killer. Before they could release the sketch, however, authorities identified the suspect as James Earl Ray from a latent fingerprint lifted off the rifle.

Ray was a convicted felon who used the alias Harvey Lowmeyer. He was a fugitive wanted for escaping from a Missouri prison. The FBI also learned that Ray had earlier obtained a California bartender's license, for which licensees were required to submit a photograph of their face, similar to those on a driver's license.

Heafner and others waited excitedly for Ray's photo to arrive. They wanted to see if his eyes had the same "steel blue" appearance described by the witnesses. Much to their dismay, when the photograph finally arrived, Ray's eyes were closed.

Regardless, a warrant was issued for Ray's arrest based on evidence obtained by authorities. He was tracked to London and arrested without incident at Heathrow Airport and extradited back to the United States. Ray was eventually sentenced to ninety-nine years in prison after pleading guilty and waiving his right to trial. Later, he recanted his confession and claimed he was part of a conspiracy involving a shadowy figure named "Raoul." He proclaimed his innocence up until the time he died, helping to fuel a variety of conspiracy theories.

And what became of Heafner's sketch? It was never released to the public because police had identified Ray so quickly and there had been no criminal trial.

Heafner said he was very relieved when Ray was caught. He said Ray's sketch could have proved difficult because his features were so generic, making it difficult for witnesses to remember his facial features or the public to connect him to the sketch.

Compounding the problem were the other sketches drawn of Ray by both local police and newspapers who commissioned their own artists to come up with a rendition of the assassin. Heafner remembers the FBI imploring the media not to release them because to do so might confuse the public and hamper the investigation. Again, because Ray was quickly identified, the sketches became a moot point.

Heafner said that had there been a trial, these other drawings would have complicated the government's case because all of them looked so different from one another.

Heafner's lengthy career allowed him to participate in other historical cases.

In the FBI's first use of hypnosis, one of many groundbreaking crime-solving methods used by the agency, Heafner was asked to sketch the faces of two kidnapping/ extortion suspects from Dallas, Texas. Although the FBI had had reservations about using hypnosis, the results proved to be a great success and illustrated the value of hypnotizing eyewitnesses in certain cases.

Heafner later summed up his career describing it as, "highly challenging." He went on to say, "The close of a case is very rewarding, and while a drawing may not directly affect its outcome, I was glad to be able to help."

Unlike the media attention bestowed upon today's sketch artists, Heafner said, he worked anonymously on many "life and death" cases that he was honored to have had the opportunity to be involved with. That's the reason he entered government service – to help people.

J. Horace Heafner passed away on March 13, 2014, in Waynesboro, Virginia. The impact he had on my career was significant and the lessons he taught me will never be forgotten.

Fernando Ponce, Los Angeles Police Department
With thousands of drawings to his credit, Fernando Ponce single-handedly papered the Los Angeles landscape with drawings of some of the city's most notorious criminals.

As his reputation grew, he became known simply by his surname, "Ponce," in an era before rock stars and other celebrities became known for adopting one-word names.

Ponce, a native of Ecuador, was a classically trained oil painter. He attended Parson's School of Design in Los Angeles and graduated with a degree in fine art.

Once while he was at city hall in Los Angeles paying a traffic ticket, he saw a Los Angeles Police Department flier seeking applicants for a police sketch artist position. He applied on a lark and successfully landed the job. Ponce once shared with me that Paul Conrad, the well-known Los Angeles Times syndicated political cartoonist, had also competed for the job.

Before long, Ponce's drawings became well-known in local law enforcement circles. For a time, he was producing approximately 700 sketches per year, making him one of the busiest police sketch artists in the country.

During our times together, he stressed having strong drawing skills and would constantly exhort me to "draw … draw … draw." He chided me for attending so many police sketch artist training courses. His advice to me was to quit going to them and just work on my own drawing skills.

Another key to Ponce's success was his skill as an interviewer. He understood people and easily connected with them. With his heavy accent and disarming personality, he had a certain charm and would address everyone he met as "my friend."

I spent much time with him as he tutored me on the

nuances of the job. People in the Scientific Investigation Division of the Los Angeles Police Department were drawn to him and he reacted with mock amusement as if he had a secret that only he knew.

Ponce was a pioneer in the field of police composite art and was always looking for ways to improve his skills. For a short time, Ponce flirted with the idea of developing composites using a computer. When the technology at that time wouldn't allow for the high quality product he was seeking, he began studying skin tone colors instead.

Soon, he was applying oil sticks to his sketches and turning out richly colored composite images. At that time, he was the only person in the country routinely producing police suspect sketches in color.

Ponce worked hard to advance our field and was a great goodwill representative to law enforcement. He worked on many memorable cases over the years, but the one that stands out above the rest is the "Night Stalker" case.

In the summer of 1985, Richard Ramirez terrorized California residents by embarking on a rape/murder spree stretching from San Francisco to southern Orange County. Law enforcement officials dubbed him the "Night Stalker" because he would sneak into people's homes at night through unlocked or open windows.

Once inside the homes, he would murder the male residents before raping, and later murdering, his female victims. In several of the victims' homes, he left behind signs of satanic worship scrawled in the victims' blood.

In a few of the cases, the victims survived these vicious attacks and helped develop composite sketches of the suspect.

Finally, it would be Ponce would draw a composite that would become the signature image of this evil incarnate. The sketch became widely publicized. Later, it became the object of criticism because during Ramirez's bloody rampage, two Los Angeles police officers stopped Ramirez and issued him a traffic citation. He was released after officers failed to make a connection between Ramirez and the widely circulated sketch.

Someone else made the connection though. A female roommate of Ramirez's later told police that she returned home during a newscast about the case. When they displayed Ponce's composite on the television screen, he remarked to her, "Do you think that looks like me?" and she dismissed him by saying, "Naw, you don't have the guts."

The woman later said that she had felt the composite was a good likeness of Ramirez and thought about calling police but hesitated, thinking, "This guy doesn't have the guts to be doing what they're describing."

My personal opinion is that the officers who stopped Ramirez and issued the citation had only one concern – traffic enforcement. In my experience, unless a crook jumped into their car, they were happy to move on to the next ticket. That is because their primary assignment was writing tickets, not arresting crooks. Would an officer whose assignment was hunting career criminals make the connection? We'll never know.

I thought there were many facial elements consistent with Ramirez's appearance. I believe the large open eyes in the composite sketch were the result of a heightened state of excitement captured by the victim's memory during the attack.

After the Night Stalker case, Ponce continued his torrid drawing pace over the next few years until his retirement.

Today, I continue to apply his teachings in my work, especially how I treat my victims and eyewitnesses. I will always remember the gleam in his eye, his cheerful grin and that knowing chuckle as he went about his business making crime-fighting appear effortless.

Tom Macris, San Jose Police Department

Few people in law enforcement have enjoyed the wide range of success that Tom Macris, San Jose Police Department's first full-time police sketch artist, experienced. Described by some in the business as a living legend and a pioneer in the field of forensic art, Macris has been credited with more felony arrests in his career than several cops put together!

Macris' career as police officer with the San Jose Police Department spanned 29 years, during which he held a variety of assignments that included patrol officer, motorcycle officer and tactical team member. He retired in 1995 as the department's police sketch artist and was succeeded by Gil Zamora, another talented artist and police officer.

His biggest contribution to law enforcement was made during his assignment as the department's first police sketch artist. It wasn't long before he became famous in the Bay Area law enforcement community for his accurate sketches and gentle approach to crime victims. His drawings, which investigators dubbed "Macrisketches," became sought-after collector's items. Like many police sketch artists, Macris had an early interest in art. As a nine-year-old budding cartoonist, he began drawing Donald Duck and continued drawing through school. In 1966, he met a police officer while studying art at San Jose State University. After spending time talking with him, he figured it was a job he could easily do. Soon after, he became a member of the San Jose Police Department.

It wasn't long before he distinguished himself as a talented cartoonist. His preparation of presentation materials for the department's training bureau caught many people's attention. One of those people was newly appointed Police Chief Joseph McNamara. After taking command of the department in 1976, McNamara wanted a staff artist who could draw police sketches like the ones he had dealt with while serving as chief of police in Kansas City, Missouri.

By that time, Macris' reputation was already established, and he was approached about taking the job. He eagerly accepted the position and soon established himself as a leader in a field that was still in its infancy. With no established standards or available training, Macris soon became the person others gravitated toward when beginning their own careers as police sketch artists. Many of us went to him early in our careers, and he was gracious enough to mentor us through our humble beginnings.

Macris found his work in the national spotlight in 1978, after a gravely wounded fifteen-year-old runaway was found wandering on a roadside in Modesto. Naked, dazed and bleeding, she had been kidnapped, raped and left for dead by her assailant after he chopped off both her hands and forearms.

Authorities called on Macris to meet with the victim, Mary Vincent, in the hospital. Despite her injuries, she was able to assist Macris in constructing a sketch of the man who had picked her up while hitchhiking and attacked her. He was later identified by authorities as Lawrence Singleton. When Macris' sketch was compared with Singleton's photograph, it bore a chilling and accurate resemblance.

Macris described his encounter with Vincent to a local newspaper as, "one of the most adverse interviews" he'd ever done. At that point in his career, he considered it a short interview at forty-five minutes.

He later explained to me that it wasn't adverse from the standpoint of Vincent's willingness to participate. Considering the level of trauma she experienced, Macris found her to be very willing. The biggest challenge for Macris was that he was only into the second year of his career as a police sketch artist and was still formulating his style and polishing his skills.

He first met Vincent in her hospital room where he worked with her on the sketch. During the interview, she was medicated and suffering a great amount of physical discomfort from her brutal and highly unusual wounds. Macris could tell she'd suffered much trauma. To compound these obstacles, there was the constant interruption from nurses coming into the room every few moments.

When the interview and sketch were completed, Macris was amazed they were able to accomplish anything at all given the circumstances. But Vincent was satisfied with the end product, even though Macris felt she was only being polite in allowing him to conduct the brief interview.

Macris' sketch thrust his work into the national spotlight given the nature of the case. It wasn't long before a woman called the police to report that the sketch greatly resembled her neighbor, Lawrence Singleton.

After his arrest, Singleton was tried and convicted in 1979 in a San Diego court for the attack on Vincent after the presentation of both physical evidence and Vincent's riveting testimony. The jury disregarded Singleton's ridiculous story about the attack, and the judge sentenced him to the maximum prison time the law would allow.

But it wouldn't be the last time anyone heard from Singleton.

After his parole and release from prison in 1987, he moved to Florida. He settled into a quiet neighborhood with people who seemed to accept him. Soon, his violent tendencies would resurface. Nine days after being released from a psychiatric facility for an attempted suicide in 1997, a deputy knocking on his door in Tampa found him with the body of a slain prostitute, Roxanne Hayes, thirty-one, a mother of three, on the floor.

Again, he was arrested and convicted. Sentenced to death in 1998, Singleton died of cancer in a Florida prison hospital three years later at age seventy-four. Though the state never got to exact its punishment, he could no longer harm anyone.

In the meantime, Macris continued working on other difficult cases. The Singleton case put him and his job on the map. Despite the high expectations to crack other cases with equal success, he never succumbed to the pressure, which Macris once told me he had learned to internalize without letting it affect him.

If you saw Tom Macris, you would experience a feeling of tranquility. He didn't look like your typical cop and didn't act like one either. Macris is tall and lean with soft, inquisitive eyes. Sporting a beard that further softens his appearance, his quiet demeanor put victims at ease and created a calming atmosphere for those around him.

Former San Jose Police Chief Lou Covarrubias described Macris as a "free-spirited intellectual." Macris was one who always relied on his intuition. He possessed a sensitivity that helped connect him with victims and eyewitnesses. The confidence Macris had in his own abilities allowed him to let the victim guide the interview. Then before completing the sketch, he showed the victim reference photographs to further reinforce and refine what they described. This added subtle nuances, resulting in greater detail. Macris' deliberate and methodical approach was a large contributor to his success.

Macris believed that people's memories for faces are incomplete. With that in mind, he saw his job as "helping them fill in the empty spaces."

Aside from those empty spaces, there was an even bigger void that Macris recognized – the lack of qualified police sketch artists. Macris knew law enforcement needed a solution to help handle all the crime that was occurring throughout the country. With computers' improving ability to produce graphic images, he wanted to build on his success by leveraging the developing technology. If Macris could get a computer to generate composite images like his, then it would go a long way toward providing law enforcement with another valuable crime-fighting tool, giving them a police sketch artist in a desktop PC. To accomplish his goal, he partnered with the Visatex Corporation in 1978 to develop and pioneer computer software that revolutionized the field of police sketching. Macris created the hand-drawn facial feature components on which the system was built.

The software, called Compu-Sketch, has since been replaced by more advanced composite imaging software. Macris retired in 1995 from the San Jose Police Department. Those of us lucky enough to have spent time with him were inspired to continue his legacy of excellence in moving the field forward.

Each of these distinguished police sketch artists possessed a different skill set that contributed to my success. And in each case, they each achieved the same result – the identification and arrest of violent criminals.

Today, there remain many highly-qualified police sketch artists working hard to distinguish themselves and mentor others. I greatly admire their work, and I wish I could have highlighted all of them.

When I stop to reflect on my own contributions to the field, I consider myself lucky to have had the opportunity to help out and make a difference. At the end of the day, like many, I consider myself an ordinary person who has an extraordinary career. But even so, I try not to spend too much time thinking about it, because it's not about me, or the rest of us, it's about those we serve.

And since crime never takes a break, neither do I. So, I better pick up my pencil and get back to work.

MICHAEL W. STREED

Chapter 15
I - Witness

Throughout this book you've read tragic stories of true crimes that happened to real people who were preyed upon by vicious criminals.

All of these victims were people just like you, your friends or loved ones. Many of these people were simply in the wrong place at the wrong time. Others were specifically targeted by a predator and never stood a chance, no matter what precautions they may have taken.

If you monitor the news with any frequency, you'll see that they were not alone. Look around -- it's happening all around us, each and every day, in every community in America.

If you don't believe me, visit the Federal Bureau of Investigation's Crime Clock, located on their website at *http://www.fbi.gov*. According to their latest violent-crime statistics, compiled in 2013, a violent crime happens every 27.1 seconds in the United States.

If those numbers are accurate that means, at this moment, while you're reading this book, someone's name is being scrawled across the front page of a police crime report or, worse yet, etched in granite to memorialize their final resting place.

Maybe you know them. Maybe one of them was you.

It's often said, "Bad things happen to good people." From my experience, I believe that's true.

However, if you closely examine how people became victims of serious crime, you'll find that in some cases, something could have been done to avoid it. Maybe the person just became complacent or overconfident. Or maybe they made a poor choice that increased their vulnerability, making them a target of opportunity.

But it doesn't have to happen that way. Taking responsibility for your own personal safety by learning to practice good, common-sense safety habits can make you more streetwise and safe.

Today, law enforcement resources are stretched thinner than ever. The police cannot be everywhere. Each one of us has to be responsible for our own safety.

This chapter is designed with you in mind. I want to help *YOU* take responsibility for *YOUR* personal safety.

In the following pages, you'll be reminded of several common-sense safety tips. You'll also be provided with tips on how to become a better witness, something that is especially important if you become the target of a violent criminal.

I also want you to be able to assist the police after you survive such an encounter. Keeping your presence of mind will help you make observations about your assailant so you can later describe the suspect to a police officer -- or maybe to a police sketch artist.

Remember that prevention is the key to combatting crime and increasing your personal safety.

If you don't know where to start, go online. Most police departments' websites have educational resources dedicated to community awareness. Check to see what local programs your local department offers. Many of them staff crime prevention units whose mission is to provide public information on safety and prevention.

Be proactive. With a few simple steps, you can learn how to protect yourself, both at home and in public.

In the next few pages, I will discuss several tips that I believe could be keep you safe. Some of them might sound familiar and will serve as a reminder. Others you might not have considered until now.

Keep in mind that a determined criminal is capable of defeating even the best defense. When that moment occurs, your determination to survive and overcome an attack must match or exceed their desire to harm you.

In my experience, most criminals would rather avoid a confrontation.

But you must also be aware that there are some who thrive on committing violence. With that in mind, you must always be careful not to place yourself in a position of jeopardy. Not paying attention to your surroundings only places you at greater risk.

Below are some recommendations I've gathered during my 35 years of professional law enforcement experience. While I cannot, and will not, guarantee your safety, I will provide you plenty of precautions to consider. How you use them, or if you choose to use them, is completely up to you.

Driving About in Public:

- Always lock your car doors.
- Know the area you are driving in and take a well-lighted, well-traveled route, especially at night. (Do not rely on popular computer mapping programs as they sometimes don't map out the safest, most

accurate route.)

- Keep your car in good mechanical condition, tires inflated, etc.
- If your car develops mechanical trouble, wait inside the locked vehicle. If someone stops to help, ask them to summon police or roadside assistance for you -- do not get out of your car.
- If you have one, carry a cellphone. (Don't rely on it alone though, as different carriers have different coverage areas.)
- Carry a fully charged flashlight inside your car. (Keep extra batteries on hand.)
- Avoid using an ATM at night. (If you must use one, select a location that is well-lit with lots of pedestrian traffic nearby.)
- Park your car in a well-lit parking area, close to your destination.
- When walking back to your car, have your keys out and ready. Clutch them in a way that you can use the protruding points of the keys as a weapon against an attacker.
- Before entering your car, quickly scan your vehicle's interior to make sure no one is hiding inside.
- Keep a supply of fresh water and snacks inside your car in case you are stranded or are trapped by a natural disaster.

There are many reasons to be out in public. Maybe you are going to work, running errands or maybe you are on your way to meet someone. This person might be a co-worker, friend or someone you recently met.

The meeting itself might be personal in nature, or maybe even professional. These days there are many ways of meeting new people, including online social media and dating websites. And even though many people treat such introductions with a more relaxed attitude, please keep a few things in mind.

Meeting New, or Maybe Not-So-New People:

- Insist on meeting in public places, even if you know the person you are meeting with.
- If it is the first time you are meeting the person, consider bringing a trusted friend along.
- Before you go, let someone know your location and the name of the person you are meeting.
- If there are security cameras in or around the business, try to sit within their field of view.
- Don't change your scheduled location without alerting someone.
- If you drink alcohol, and I don't recommend you do, keep your drink close to you and DO NOT leave it unattended.
- All of the above applies to people you meet online – and especially them.
- Try to learn as much about them before meeting.
- TRUST YOUR GUT INSTINCTS!

Now, maybe you don't like going out, or, if you are like me, you just enjoy time at home with family and friends. Even so, you are still vulnerable. Luckily there are some things you can do to safeguard yourself and create a safe environment.

When at Home:

- Never forget the first rule -- ALWAYS lock your doors (even during the daytime).
- If you leave your windows open for ventilation,

secure them with a stick so the windows cannot be forced open. You might also consider placing screws in the upper or lower tracks to prevent someone from lifting the window out, or sliding them open.

- At night, maintain nighttime security or perimeter lighting.
- Keep trees and shrubbery trimmed back to prevent blocking your doors and windows from the view of a neighbor or a passing police car.
- If you have an alarm, keep it set while home and away.
- Install a peephole in your front door, or look out a side window when someone comes to the door.
- Do not open the door for anyone you do not know.
- Have a "buddy" system with your neighbors.
- Do not confront suspicious persons – instead report them to police.
- If you ever return home and it appears that someone has burglarized your home, do not enter. Go to a neighbor's where you can watch your house while you call police.
- Carefully consider whether or not you are comfortable keeping a weapon inside your home. If you are not prepared to take someone's life, a weapon is of no use to you.

I am sure there are many other considerations you have thought of that I failed to mention. That's fine, because safety is a personal matter. What works for one person might not work for another. Talk to one another, talk to your family members. Develop a safety plan because, even in the best of circumstances, the worst can happen.

Remember that any one of us can become the victim of a crime. It's even happened to me.

In October 2014, I was working downtown at the Baltimore Police Department's Crime Laboratory. My apartment was in the northern part of the city in what was considered to be one of the city's "low-crime" areas.

On my way home, I decided to stop for a cup of coffee and unwind from the day. Little did I know, while I was blissfully sipping my coffee, my apartment was being ransacked by a burglar who a witness told police was armed with a handgun.

The apartment was a small studio, located in the back of the building, facing a wooded area. Knowing that my location was isolated, I took steps to secure my windows with sticks and screws. Yet despite my best efforts, the burglar was still able to force his way into my apartment by prying at and pushing in the window, which he pretty much had all day to do because of my apartment's location.

His efforts were rewarded when he was able to force open the window just enough to reach through and unlock my front door, gaining entry to my home.

I knew that the location of my apartment was less than ideal. But at the time I rented it there was a limited selection of apartments in the area so I had to take what I could get and make the best from a not-so-ideal circumstance.

When I arrived home later, I was sickened to find that my apartment had been trashed. The incident left me with an unsettled feeling. Although I stayed there for several days, I eventually moved because there had been things inside that identified me as a member of law enforcement. And while I hated the fact that someone was dictating my lifestyle, I can only think of what might have happened had I not moved, or if I had come home a few minutes earlier and wound up confronting the armed burglar.

For some reason, he targeted my residence and hit the jackpot. So you see, even police officers, or retired police officers, can become crime victims too.

I shared this personal story because it highlights my earlier point that there always will be criminals who are committed to preying upon you and defeating your defenses.

And while we are on the topic of residential crimes, let's talk about sexual assaults that occur if an attacker gets inside the home.

During my career, I've been called upon to investigate such attacks or interview courageous survivors who were able to assist me in creating a sketch of the suspect. These crimes are frightening and traumatic events that are always difficult to tackle because of social and cultural implications.

Many of these survivors I found to be strong people who, with the proper support, turn tragedy into triumph. Initially, they can feel powerless, their lives shattered, because they feel abandoned or isolated by those they trust most for support, which can lead to their lacking trust in anybody.

It's an uncomfortable situation for many who are not emotionally equipped to deal with the aftermath of crimes. Sometimes, those who want to help wind up alienating the survivor by making them feel responsible for something they were powerless to stop.

Luckily there's hope for them. Survivors of sexual assault have a tremendous amount of power and *can* fight back. To do this, they must assist law enforcement by providing an accurate and timely account of the facts.

By remaining engaged with police and prosecutors, survivors can effectively aid in the investigation and prosecution of crimes committed against them. The only caveat is, there is no guarantee that along the way circumstances may prevent charges from being filed or a jury may acquit an accused person. But, without cooperation, there is little the criminal justice system can do to help them ensure justice.

In the aftermath of such grave crimes, I offer some recommendations for survivors:

- Review the safety tips earlier in the chapter.
- Do not minimize your importance to the investigation. Your value as an eyewitness is critical. During the attack:
  - o Remain calm and maintain a presence of mind.
  - o Try to remember as many details as possible.
  - o Write them down, or record them on your phone as soon as possible.
- Immediately report the crime to police, or disclose to someone you trust.
  - o This person, or an advocate, may call the police for you and remain with you through the process.
  - o The collection and preservation of evidence is key. You should not delay reporting!
  - o Evidence degrades over time, or it can be lost or destroyed.
- It is normal to be upset and/or confused. Psychologically, a survivor may feel "dirty" and will try to cleanse themselves by showering and changing clothes. This can destroy biological evidence and must be avoided until authorities have processed clothing and other evidence.

Please remember that it's important to preserve all evidence. DNA identification technology continues to develop and has become key to successfully identifying suspects and prosecuting sexual assault cases years after they were committed.

Many states are adopting laws that require state prison inmates to submit a biological sample for genetic coding prior to their release or during their incarceration. Some have even contributed DNA samples in exchange for lesser sentences for misdemeanor crimes in county courts.

This has become helpful to jurisdictions that use the information to expand local or statewide databases, which have been combined and shared throughout the United States. This has contributed greatly to the identification and arrest of suspects who would have otherwise remained unidentified.

Still, supplementing any DNA evidence, or sometimes standing on its own, will always be eyewitness identification.

I know that eyewitness identification has been characterized by defense attorneys and academic researchers as unreliable and also that DNA has been used to exonerate suspects convicted by the word of an eyewitness. But even so, we still continue to depend on such information, even though. That's because in many instances eyewitnesses get it right and make good identifications, which reinforces that eyewitness identification remains an important law enforcement tool that should still be carefully used.

Sometimes memories can be fleeting and over time become fuzzy. This results in a breakdown in the eyewitness's confidence. Over time, outside influences combined with other factors can act to erode the reliability of eyewitness identification.

Still, I still think eyewitnesses remain an important part of the criminal justice system. To help them become more reliable sources of information we must work with academics and other experts to find better ways to document and report what we see.

And because many still recognize its importance, research into eyewitness identification continues around the world at many well-respected universities and new discoveries are being reported.

In the meantime, don't be afraid to come forward. Protect

your memory to the best of your ability and help protect and preserve any physical evidence. This will help keep you ahead of the game and assist you with taking back your life when it's time to seek justice.

In reality, all crimes rely on eyewitness reporting and identification. I interview eyewitnesses on a daily basis and have found them to be an earnest sort, who can sometimes be reluctant to engage with police. They are often reluctant to commit because they are afraid of being wrong and possibly sending an innocent person to jail. I get that. I wouldn't want to carry that burden either. But I think it is our civic duty to stand up and do the right thing, including cooperating with police.

Whether a person comes into my office or talks to me on the phone, there are two things I'm consistently told: A) It happened fast, and B) It was dark.

That doesn't surprise me at all. I always tell them that they only way a suspect is going to stop and pose in a well-lit area, long enough to be identified, is while their booking photo is taken. That usually causes them to pause for a moment and think about it and then, they are ready to begin the interview.

I think in my role as a police sketch artist and interviewer it is important to manage expectations. To help with that, I would suggest the following to victims and eyewitnesses.

- First, a witness or victim must trust their own observations, even if others don't.
- One of the first keys to a successful identification is for the eyewitness to realize they are witnessing a crime. (Unfortunately, in some cases, people don't realize what they are witnessing until later.)
- You must have the presence of mind to remain calm in the face of danger and experience all that is going on around you.

- Research supports that memory begins to fade over time and, in fact, often begins to degrade immediately. It is important to write down or tape record your observations and impressions as soon as it is practical. These notes will help to later refresh your memory at the time you must give a statement to law enforcement. Some suggest people carry a pocket tape recorder or small notepad and pen at all times. Improving cellphone technology means those devices also can serve that purpose.
- Move yourself away from others while you record your observations. This will avoid any innocent collusion of perceptions from those around you who may or may not have seen the crime themselves. Try later to minimize your exposure to media accounts and "man on the street" opinion polls and sound bites. Family and friends may try to give you their bias-laced opinions, but try not to engage in such discussions. This is the time when most memory contamination occurs.
- When you are describing someone's height and weight don't be afraid to use someone nearby as a visual reference. Use the officer or investigator themselves. People are visual learners and most learn faster through demonstration, even when they are the ones doing the demonstrating.
- When it comes to describing a suspect's face, don't be afraid to compare their facial features and expressions with someone familiar to you, even if it's a movie star or other famous person.
- Don't forget, though, when observing someone's face, to concentrate on features that are "anchored" to the face, such as the nose, eyes, and mouth. These are important facial landmarks that remain static and

are not likely to change. Hairstyles and facial hair oftentimes are the features most often changed to disguise someone's appearance.

- Cross-racial identification can become a barrier when asking someone to later identify an attacker. Although we can recall details about facial features, when a suspect is viewed in a lineup with others of the same race at the same time, for example, witnesses of another race can have trouble differentiating one individual from another.

Afterward, it is important to return to your normal life as you begin the healing phase. The ability to talk about the crime and share it with others becomes important.

The person you choose to share your experience with must be an active listener. They must have compassion and be willing to help you get through the most difficult time in your life. For some this can be a life-altering event that causes positive changes to take place. I always tell people to keep talking about what happened, until even you are sick of hearing yourself talk about it. After that, you can move on with your life.

Remember that once you report a crime to police, you have met your obligation -- stay engaged in the process though and remain cooperative, but leave it up to law enforcement to follow up your observations and try to corroborate them. If everything goes well and everybody does their job, your observations will lead to evidence that points toward a suspect and JACKPOT! -- an arrest can be made and hopefully, a successful prosecution will follow.

But if there is no evidence and it's left up to you because as an eyewitness, you *are* the best evidence, then it is up to prosecutors to put on the best case possible with just your statement. Keep in mind, though, it is ultimately the prosecutor's decision on whether or not to proceed, or to wait until police come up with further corroborating evidence.

An example of this often occurs in cold case murder investigations. A suspect is developed early during the investigation, but there isn't enough evidence to prosecute until years later. And though it can be frustrating to the families of victims, the legal process is something we should respect as part of the constitutional protections that are afforded to each and every one of us.

It's easy to point a finger and blame someone else. Sometimes, even with the best intention, the system fails us and we can become disillusioned.

As a lifelong member of the criminal justice system, I understand those feelings and I am sympathetic to each person's struggle. Sometimes we like to think we are the only ones who have been affected by crime, but we are not.

Throughout the chapter I have tried hard to avoid using the word "victim." It is a term I despise because it makes us sound weak and helpless. Trust me, we are not the helpless ones. It is the predatory criminal who is weak. We are anything but helpless. I know that there are more good people out there than bad ones. If all the good people rose up without fear against the criminals, the world would be a much safer place.

My personal belief has always been that with a positive attitude and strong support, tragedy *can* be turned into triumph. Each tragedy we suffer and how we react become the building blocks of our character.

As humans, we carry the will to survive deep inside of us. When attacked, our minds become powerful tools that drive our bodies to perform great feats of strength.

Having that power allows us to become our most effective weapon against crime because, to win the battle against crime, you must always fight back against it.

And when you do that, we *ALL* win!

For More *SketchCop* Photos and Sketches
http://wbp.bz/sketchcopgallery

Use this link to sign up for advance notice
of Michael W. Streed's Next Book:
http://wildbluepress.com/AdvanceNotice

Word-of-mouth is critical to an author's long-term success.
If you appreciated this book please leave a review on the
Amazon sales page:
http://wbp.bz/sketchcopreviews

**Coming to WildBlue Press and
Investigation Discovery in February**

A TASTE FOR MURDER

BY

BURL BARER AND FRANK GIRARDOT

PRE-ORDER YOUR COPY NOW AT OUR SPECIAL PRE-LAUNCH PRICE OF 99 CENTS!

Frank Garcia, a much-loved counselor of troubled teens, lies dead on the bedroom floor. His wife and step-daughter are in shock, and so is the medical examiner when he performs the autopsy. Aside from being dead, Frank is in perfect health. Demanding to know the cause of her husband's death, Angie Garcia badgers the police, insisting that he was murdered. The cops attribute her assertions to overwhelming grief, but soon they too believe that Frank didn't die of natural causes. When the police enlist their number one suspect to help in the investigation, things spiral out of control until police are dealing with a daring plot to murder Angie's best friend and allegations of another homicide so evil and perverse that even seasoned L.A County Detectives are shocked beyond belief. Edgar Award winner Burl Barer teams with famed crime journalist Frank C. Girardot, Jr to bring you a true story so bizarre and disturbing that Investigation Discovery devoted a full hour to exploring this epic mystery - A TASTE FOR MURDER.

Read More About A TASTE FOR MURDER At:
http://wbp.bz/atasteformurder
www.WildBluePress.com

WINNER OF THE SUSPENSE MAGAZINE BEST TRUE CRIME OF 2015

Repeat Offender by Bradley Nickell
www.WildBluePress.com

REPEAT OFFENDER
BRADLEY NICKELL with WARREN JAMISON

Millions in stolen property, revolting sex crimes and murder-for-hire were all in the mix for a Las Vegas police detective as he toiled to take Sin City's most prolific criminal off the streets for good.

In REPEAT OFFENDER Las Vegas Police Detective Bradley Nickell brings you the inside scoop on the investigation of the most prolific repeat offender Las Vegas has ever known.

Daimon Monroe looked like an average guy raising a family with his diffident schoolteacher girlfriend. But just below the surface, you'll learn he was an accomplished thief with an uncontrollable lust for excess. His criminal mind had no bounds—he was capable of anything given the proper circumstances.

You will be revolted by Monroe's amassed wealth through thievery, his plot to kill Detective Nickell, a judge and a prosecutor, and the physical and sexual abuse to which Monroe subjected his daughters.

Read More About REPEAT OFFENDER At:
www.WildBluePress.com

**More True Crime You'll Love
From WildBlue Press.**

Learn more at: http://wbp.bz/tc

More Mysteries/Thrillers You'll Love From WildBlue Press.

Learn more at: http://wbp.bz/cf

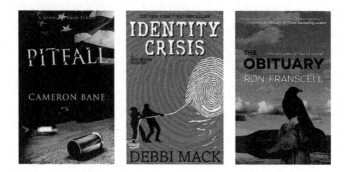

www.WildBluePress.com

Go to WildBluePress.com to sign up for our newsletter!

By subscribing to our newsletter you'll get *advance notice* of all new releases as well as notifications of all special offers. And you'll be registered for our monthly chance to win a **FREE collection of our eBooks and/or audio books** to some lucky fan who has posted an honest review of our one of our books/eBooks/audio books on Amazon, Itunes and GoodReads.

Let Someone Else Do The Reading.
Enjoy One Of Our Audiobooks

Learn more at: http://wbp.bz/audio

**Please feel free to check out more True CRIME books
by our friends at**

www.RJPARKERPUBLISHING.com

CPSIA information can be obtained
at www.ICGtesting.com
Printed in the USA
LVOW13s0634240517

535631LV00007B/196/P